Archibald Hook, Charles Collins Campbell, Harriet Fraser Campbell

Major Hook's Defence

To the Action or Criminal Conversation, Brought Against him by Capt. Charles

Campbell

Archibald Hook, Charles Collins Campbell, Harriet Fraser Campbell

Major Hook's Defence
To the Action or Criminal Conversation, Brought Against him by Capt. Charles Campbell

ISBN/EAN: 9783337139841

Printed in Europe, USA, Canada, Australia, Japan

Cover: Foto ©Suzi / pixelio.de

More available books at **www.hansebooks.com**

'MAJOR HOOK's

DEFENCE,

TO THE

ACTION

OR

CRIMINAL CONVERSATION,

BROUGHT AGAINST HIM

BY

CAPT. CHARLES CAMPBELL,

AND

TRIED AT WESTMINSTER,

26th February, 1793.

LONDON:

PRINTED FOR J. MURRAY, FLEET-STREET.
1793.

ADVERTISEMENT.

THIS defence contains obfervations upon the teftimony of the witneffes on whofe evidence the verdict againft me was found, and on a variety of evidence contained in affidavits and letters, which are annexed at length in the appendix, to which the defence refers. It is thought proper likewife to annex an account of the trial taken in fhort hand, by Mr. Blanchard, becaufe the defence neceffarily refers to the trial, and cannot be underftood without it.

DEFENCE.

IT will naturally occur to the reader, that if I had had a defence by which I could have proved my innocence, I would have brought it forwards at the trial. In anfwer to this I have to fay, that moft of the material facts of which the prefent defence confifts, were contained in the inftructions given to my counfel; whether all the obfervations upon thefe facts contained in the following fheets occurred to them, I cannot pretend to fay. Indeed, I fhould be very much furprifed if men, even of the talents which my counfel are univerfally allowed to poffefs, could embrace in the inftant every thing that might occur upon mature confideration of the fubject. And I would farther remark, that although the arguments and obfervations might not occur at once, it does not

follow,

follow, therefore, that they are lefs grounded in truth, or conclufive in reafon.

No perfon can hold in higher refpect than I do, the invaluable privilege of trial- by jury. But with the moft perfect attachment and veneration for that inftitution, I may remark, that it will happen that fome cafes might be better tried by a more deliberate mode of inquiry; and that pre-judices will fometimes be created in the courfe of a trial by jury, which more temperate difcuf-fions would prevent or remove. But as on the one hand, I by no means intend to infinuate, that becaufe a few cafes may be mifguided by that form of trial, that, that is an argument againft the inftitution : fo, on the other hand, if by deli-berate inveftigation and difcuffion, I can make out my cafe, and prove my innocence, it will not be faid, that I am lefs intitled to the effect of a deliberate and extrajudicial juftification.

The public and my friends will not be furprifed, if in vindication of my character, fo deeply and feverely wounded by the verdict given againft me in this action, I fhould take this method of of-fering my defence to their confideration.

I am

I am impelled to this meafure by every motive which can operate upon the mind of man.

'The protection I owe to the innocent and injured reputation of a young woman, whom I am bound by all the ties of parental affinity to fupport under circumftances of the moft afflicting adverfity. The duty of a parent to hand down his reputation unfullied to his children, as their beft inheritance and fureft fecurity for virtue, and the regard I have for my own character, which, I am bold to fay, has been uniformly moral, pure, and upright, all induce me to make this appeal to the candour and judgement of an impartial public; and I am left, indeed, without any other means, at prefent, of vindicating myfelf, becaufe I underftand that the rules of law will not, in the circumftances I ftand, admit of my obtaining a new trial, whatever may be the actual merits of my cafe.

Before I proceed to ftate the facts and arguments on which I reft my innocence, I feel it incumbent on me moft diftinctly to declare, that I do not mean, in what I fhall fay, to impute the flighteft blame to the jury who found the verdict, or to the noble and learned Judge who prefided at the trial of the caufe : on the contrary, I admit

that

that the observations made by the judge, and the verdict given by the jury, were the natural result of the impressions made at the time, by the positive testimony of the witnesses.

But I have many observations to make which will, I trust, upon deliberate consideration, repel these impressions ; and I have many facts to state, supported by affidavits, which will give a very different complexion to my case, insomuch, that I have no doubt of convincing the world of that innocence, which I am ready to protest under all the sanctions which religion can impose.

It will appear from the annexed account of the trial, that the case opened for the plaintiff, by Mr. Erskine, was a case of deliberate seduction, calculated by a long train of artful address, well-contrived opportunities, and indecent incitements, to make a young person, to whom I stood in the relation of a parent, and to whom I owed all the duties of parental affection, yield to my base designs upon her virtue.*

The evidence produced was meant to support the case thus opened by the plaintiff's counsel.

* Appendix, p. 59, E.

It

It is by no means neceſſary for the eſtabliſh-
ment of guilt, of the ſort in queſtion, either to
ſtate or prove a deliberate plan of ſeduction ; but
if a ſyſtem of ſeduction is laid down as the ground-
work of the crime, and is propoſed to be made
out by evidence, it is eſſentially neceſſary to the
truth of the charge ſo made, that there ſhould be
a conformity in the evidence to the nature of the
caſe propoſed to be made out, and that there
ſhould be a conſiſtency in the evidence with
itſelf; and it is fair to draw this concluſion, that if
the evidence eſtabliſhes, or aims at eſtabliſhing in
part, a caſe totally inconſiſtent with ſeduction,
opened and reſted upon by the plaintiff, ſuch evidence not only removes the ground on which the
guilt is meant to be founded, but deſtroys the
credit due to it, both as founded on ſeduction,
and as founded on the very facts which repel the
preſumption of ſeduction.

The doctrine here laid down cannot be more
perfectly illuſtrated than by the caſe which gave
riſe to the verdict under which I now ſuffer.

I returned from India, as has been repreſented
in the cauſe, in the month of July, 1788 ; I had
reſided there for one and twenty years, with the
exception of a viſit to England of a few months

in

in the year 1773. Mrs. Campbell was about 18 years of age when I returned to England in 1788, and I had never feen her from her birth but once, when an infant in arms, at Madras, where fhe was with her father and mother, at the time of my voyage to and from England, in 1773.

She was confequently, as fhe has been defcribed, an abfolute ftranger to me on my arrival in London, at which time fhe was at her mother's houfe in Brook-ftreet, my refidence being at Kenfington with my children.

I had at that time, as appears from the opening of the plaintiff's cafe, but few opportunities of feeing her, for fhe went fhortly after my arrival in England with her mother to Ramfgate.

It is ftated that I went to Ramfgate in September,* and joined the family with an intention of taking her to Scotland, on the pretence of feeing her relations, but in reality to accomplifh the bafe purpofe of feducing her from a hufband with whom fhe is reprefented by his two brothers, Mr. Donald, and Lawrence Campbell, and the wife of the latter gentleman, to have lived in a ftate of perfect domeftic happinefs.

* Appendix, p. 59, G. H. 60, A.

This

This story, thus told, is a confistent tale, bearing the mark of probability.

If the depraved nature of a man, standing in the relation of a parent to the object of his illicit desires, of an age nearly passed the middle period of life, had imagined to himself the diabolical purpose of seducing a girl of eighteen years of age, he might have contrived some such scheme of exclusive intercourse and familiarity as the journey of Scotland.

It is most material to my exculpation, therefore, to discover how far the evidence in the cause supports the case relied upon, and stated by the counsel for the plaintiff.

The witnesses against me swear positively to acts, situations, and expressions ; to this I mean to oppose an examination of their evidence, by the laws of probability, and the evidence of witnesses contradicting their testimony ; and believe I do not hazard an extraordinary position, when I assert, that the credit due to positive testimony may be overset by the improbability of the circumstances, and their incompatibility with any rational system of belief.

The

The examination of Elizabeth Herbſon, the firſt witneſs called to prove the fact of my guilt, was as follows :—" * Q. I believe you lived a cook " with Mrs. Fraſer? A. I did. Q. Were you " in that capacity with her in the year 1788 ? " A. Yes, Sir, I was. Q. Do you remember " the family going to Ramſgate in the year 1788? " A. Yes, Sir, I do. Q. How long was that " after Major Hook's arrival—do you remember " in what month ? A. I believe it was in July, " Q. Mrs. Fraſer went to Ramſgate? A. Yes, " Q. And Mrs. Campbell ? A. Yes. Q. Was " Major Hook there? A. He was not. Q. He " came there after you went ? A. Yes, he did; " Q. Where was Captain Campbell ? A. I be= " lieve at Chatham or Portſmouth. Q. Was he " with his regiment there ? A. I cannot ſay. " How long were they at Ramſgate ? A. I be= " lieve ten weeks. Q. Do you remember ſeeing " any thing particular between Mrs. Campbell and " Major Hook ? A. Never but once, Sir, when " I went in with a bit of bread. Q. When you " went in where? A. To the parlour. Q. What " did you ſee there ? A. I ſaw the Major ſitting " with his arm round her neck, and his right leg " upon her lap. Q. Did you obſerve any

* Appendix, p. 69. D.

" thing

" thing refpecting her hair ?* A. Yes, Sir, her
" hair was rolled round his arm. Q. State what
" you faw? A. Her hair was rolled round his
" arm, his left arm. Q. Did you obferve any
" thing farther? A. His right hand in her hand-
" kerchief. *Lord Chief Juftice.* Q. The hand-
" kerchief that covered her neck? A. Yes,
" *Counfel.* Q. Did you obferve any thing elfe?
" A. No, Sir, I did not. Q. Do you remember
" Major Hook's arrival at Ramfgate? A. Yes,
" Sir, I do. Q. Did any thing particular pafs at
" the time? A. † Mrs. Campbell was very much
" alarmed, and fainted away upon his coming in;
" I remember that, Sir. Q. That you remem-
" ber? A. Yes, Sir. *Lord Chief Juftice.* Q. At
" whofe coming there? A. At Major Hook's,
" the defendant's. *Counfel.* Q. Where did they
" return again from Ramfgate? A. To Brook-

* This was furely a leading queftion, and objectionable
in the ftrongeft degree, as it pointed precifely to the witnefs what anfwer to give, which is the ground on which
leading queftions are illegal.

† Mrs. Frafer, Mrs. Campbell's mother, is now in
India; when there is the means of obtaining her teftimony, fhe will prove that this agitation arofe from her
having, for the purpofe of furprifing her daughter, in-
troduced my brother to her from Jamaica, fuddenly and
unexpectedly.

" ftreet,

" ftreet. Q. To Mrs. Frafer's? A. Yes, to the
" houfe they came from. Q. Did they all come
" together? A. No, I believe the Major went to
" his houfe. Q. You returned? A. Yes. Q. To
" Brook-ftreet, Mrs. Frafer's houfe? A. Yes.
" Q. Major Hook went to his own houfe? A.
" Yes. Q. What time was it you faw that at
" Ramfgate you have been defcribing? A. It
" was fome time in the morning. Q. In what
" month? A. I cannot fay. Q. You faid you
" went there in July? A. Yes, I believe it was
" about Michaelmas time. Q. How long was it
" before you returned to town? A. We came to
" town fome time in September. *Crofs-examined*
" *by Mr.* Bearcroft. Q. What was your fitua-
" tion in the family? A. A cook. Q. You went
" by order to the parlour? A. No, I went to
" carry a bit of bread by Mrs. Frafer's order,
" Q. For whom? A. For Mrs. Campbell and
" Major Hook. Q. They took as if they ex-
" pected it? A. I do not know whether they
" expected it or not. Q. You carried it and gave
" it them? A. I did not look at them when I
" gave the plate. Q. You went for the purpofe
" of carrying the bread there, and it was received?
" A. Yes. Q. Nobody faid for what it was fent?
" No. Q. It was expected therefore? A. Yes.
" Q. The door was open when you went in?
" A.

" A. Yes, Sir, it was. Q. Was it quite open ?
" A. *Partly open.* Q. You delivered the bread
" and went away; you did not stay, I suppose ?
" A. I did not stop a moment, hardly. Q. You
" stepp'd in and delivered the bread and went
" away ? A. Yes. Q. Did you stop at all ?
" A. No. Q. Did you let the plate fall ? A.
" No, I held it so, and one of them took it,
" I don't know which. Q. Did you not ex-
" press any particular surprize ? A. Why; I
" cannot say I liked to see them. Q. You made
" all those observations ? A. Yes. Q. Of course
" you thought it very improper ? A. Very, Sir.
" Q. Did you ever see Mr. Campbell, the huf-
" band, after that ? A. I believe I did see him
" once, he came in the hall once ; I don't re-
" collect I ever saw him but once after that. Q. I
" take it for granted you told Mrs. Frafer, the
" mother, immediately ? A. No, I did not, Sir.
" Mr. *Holroyd.* Q. How came you to take the
" bread up ? A. Mrs. Frafer ordered me to carry
" the bread. *Lord Chief Juftice.* She said so
" before. Q. Where was Mrs. Frafer ? A. She
" was in one parlour, and the Major and Mrs.
" Campbell in the other."

The fituation here defcribed, if it could be
fuppofed to have exifted at all, leads to a proof of

c   criminal

criminal intercourfe ; but it is totally inconfiftent with a plan of feduction for the purpofe of a criminal end, and confequently muft be held to repel the foundation of the general tenor of the charge, by raifing a decifive prefumption of its falfity ; a prefumption which increafes to abfolute conviction, when the evidence is examined by the ftandard of probability.

The pofitive evidence is, that within a day of my arrival at Ramfgate, where I only refided three days in all, I was found by the witnefs, Mrs. Frafer's Cook, in the parlour, with the door open, in a fituation of the groffeft indecency, fuch a perfon of the moft profligate habits could not be fuppofed to be found in with the moft abandoned proftitute. And yet this fituation, according to the cafe opened by the plaintiff's counfel, is fuppofed to have taken place between a young woman of 18, and a man of 40 years of age, between perfons who were totally ftrangers, till within a very fhort time before the fituation fworn. It proceeds upon the fuppofition that all the natural feelings of relationfhip, as well as difparity of years, were overcome in this fhort period ;* and that all this took

* Appendix, p. 63 to 69.

place

place in the cafe of a female, who, according to the evidence of the plaintiff's neareft relations, lived at that time happily with her hufband, infomuch, that a long train of fubfequent feduction is fuppofed to have been neceffary, firft to debauch her mind, and afterwards to obtain her perfonal favour. To increafe the improbability, this feene is fuppofed to have been in the middle of the day, in a parlour, in a lodging-houfe at Ramfgate, with the door *partly open*, Mrs. Frafer fitting in the oppofite parlour, and giving orders to the fervant to carry in fome bread to Mrs. Campbell and me, and the parties are fuppofed, one or other of them, to have taken a piece of bread from the witnefs, but which fhe could not tell.

Such a place, for fuch a fituation, is very little marked with probability, efpecially in a lodging-houfe, and in a watering place, where familiarity of intercourfe and accefs to the apartments is, from the eafe of living in fuch places, conftantly open to all the family; and it is inconfiftent with every rule of probability, that under thefe circumftances, they fhould have coolly and deliberately taken the bread, without moving from their fituation or pofition.

It can hardly be doubted, therefore, positive as the testimony is, that it is to be rejected as unworthy of belief—because it establishes a case inconsistent with the future plans and measures to seduce an innocent woman and beloved wife; and because it is in itself incompatible with those probabilities, on which the belief of all human testimony, however sanctioned, must depend.

The next part of this extraordinary case relates to the journey to Scotland, which I am supposed to have proposed, as affording an opportunity to corrupt Mrs. Campbell's virtue, already, according to the account of the last witness, completely corrupted; and to aggravate the wickedness of that act, and render my scheme more practicable,* I am supposed to have used means to foment a quarrel that subsisted between Captain Campbell and his father.

As these circumstances were not proved, but rested merely upon the assertion of the plaintiff's counsel, I might be allowed to pass them by with observing that they remain unproved. But I cannot permit so vile a slander to rest even in assertion, and as the learned counsel could speak only from

* Appendix, p. 60, B. C. D.

the

the inftructions of his client, it is moft important to my vindication to expofe the character which could give fuch inftructions, with a confciouf-nefs of their falfehood, of which confcioufnefs I fhall convict him, by the evidence of his own letters. And it is equally important, that I fhould eftablifh the real motives and inducements which led me to take that journey with Mrs. Campbell, as my companion.

Soon after my arrival in England, and long be-fore my journey to Ramfgate, and confequently before I am charged with any defign upon Mrs. Campbell's virtue,* I wrote to Captain Camp-bell, whofe father was my uncle, expreffive of my wifh to reconcile him to his father, with whom he had been at variance, fignifying to him my wifh that he fhould accompany me to Scot-land, previous to his departure for India, he be-ing about to embark with his regiment for that quarter of the globe. His letter,† dated the 27th day of Auguft, proves the fact as I have ftated it, and eftablifhes without the evidence of my letter, to which it was an anfwer, that taking Mrs. Campbell with me, was not propofed by

* Appendix, p. 16, 17.
† Appendix, p. 18.

me

me, nor even in my thoughts, for his letter contains no obfervations upon any fuch propofition.
Captain Campbell's letter, of the 30th of Auguft,
1788, fhews that I ftill continued to prefs him
to the journey, which he continued for various
reafons to decline ; and in this letter, he himfelf
fuggefts the idea for the firft time it ever occurred, that Mrs. Campbell fhould accompany me
to Scotland.

After ftating at large his grounds for declining
the journey himfelf, he fays,* " I hope, after
" this, you will not afk me to go to Scotland,
" when, independent of my firft reafons, the
" ftate of my regiment renders it incompatible
" for me to get away, *nor is there one fingle of-*
" *ficer of the regiment abfent with leave.*

" Mrs. Campbell, fome time ago, had a wifh
" to fee her friends in that part of the world,
" and, perhaps, if it would not be inconvenient,
" fhe would like to go as far as Edinburgh : but
" on this fubject I muft refer you to herfelf en-
" tirely ; for my own part, I am not partial to
" that country, having been but little in it, nor
" have I a defire of feeing it, unlefs to fee my
" fifter, whom I believe to be a good woman."

* Appendix 18, H. 19, A. B.

This

This letter containing the proposal, was, as I have observed, anterior to the suppofition of my having any intercourse with Mrs. Campbell, for she went to Ramfgate foon after my arrival in London. Combining the letters with the time at which they were written, the plan fuppofed to be laid me by me for the feduction of Mrs. Campbell by the journey to Scotland, is thus completely refuted, and proved to have originated with Captain Campbell himfelf.

The extraordinary proceeding of the plaintiff in the fequel will be beft feen, and his character moft completely unfolded, by his father's letters and his own, contained in the appendix.

Notwithftanding his propofal that I fhould carry his wife to Scotland, it appears from his letters that fome extraordinary caprice had induced him to quit his regiment without leave,* to poft after Mrs. Campbell. It appears that when he had got within a ftage of her aunt's houfe, in the county of Argyle, at whofe houfe we were, upon our return to London, after a vifit of four days to his father and our other friends, in the town,

* Appendix, p. 4, E. to p. 10, A. p. 26, A. to p. 23, B.

3

of

of Campbell-town, he wrote a letter to his wife from the inn, calumniating his father as an adulterer, expreſſing a kind of dark ſuſpicion of me,* and uſing the moſt violent language towards her.

It became neceſſary for me to communicate the extraordinary meaſure of this journey to his father, whoſe letter to me, in anſwer to that communication, will ſhew the reconciling ſpirit in which I had repreſented the conduct of his ſon ;† and it will hardly be ſuppoſed, if my object had been an inceſtuous intrigue with my own niece, that I ſhould have choſen, as the ſcene of my depravity, the boſom of the families of our neareſt and deareſt relations, and the center of a populous town like Campbell-town. Beſides, it is to be remarked, that there is not in the whole evidence an attempt to trace actual guilt at that period, and on that occaſion ; though no pains has been ſpared to inveſtigate my conduct, and trace my proceedings during the period of five years, throughout England, Scotland, and Wales ; and although Captain Campbell followed cloſe upon our heels, traced us in our journey from

* Appendix, p. 9, B.
† Appendix, p. 25, to 31.

ſtage

ftage to ftage through England and Scotland, and
that at a time when, from his own letters, I muft
have conceived that he *could not quit his regiment.*

If I was to have aimed at familiarity with Mrs.
Campbell at all, it may be fuppofed that I might
have confidered myfelf in a fituation of fecurity to
have done it upon this journey. I do not therefore affume too much if I fay, that as his induftry
then, and that of his agents fince, have not difcovered any evidence of it, the want of proof is,
in fuch a cafe, decifive of the non-exiftence of
the fact. It is farther to be remarked, that if the
profligate familiarity fworn to by the cook at
Ramfgate had been true, a fimilar conduct would
have been traceable in the journey to Scotland,
in all the actual and fuppofed fecurity of that
journey ; and that its not being traced, is another
proof of the falfehood of the evidence.

His letters written after his return from Scotland, while they prove the moft unreafonable and
wavering difpofition, fufficiently refute the imputation which his letter upon his arrival at the
inn in Argylefhire may feem to convey againft
me ; and, indeed, thofe letters difplay a mind fo
deformed by unreafonable and *unnatural* fufpi-
cions, as to make even the *female* friends of Mrs.

d   Camp-

Campbell the object of his intemperate paſſion and jealous expreſſions. It will not be wondered at, therefore, if at one time his letters * ſhould have the appearance of jealouſy of me, and if others, written about the ſame time, ſhould ſtate me *as the innocent cauſe of his everlaſting wretch-edneſs.*

The letters will prove that we returned to London about the 20th of November, when I left Mrs. Campbell at her mother's houſe in Brook-ſtreet, and that her huſband lived with her until the firſt of December, when he left her, and remained in England till the 8th of March following, as his letters ſhew. Upon thoſe letters, I ſhall have occaſion to obſerve hereafter; at preſent, I ſhall purſue my examination of the witneſſes in the order in which they gave their evidence upon the trial.

Joſeph Rippington † was the witneſs next called.—It appears from his evidence, that he came into my ſervice when I was at the Bath Hotel, Piccadilly, in May, 1789; that I remained there about three weeks, and then went to reſide in

* Appendix, p. 5, C.
† Appendix, p. 73, C.

Sack-

Sackville-ftreet, where, he fays, I refided nearly three months. This witnefs does not attempt to prove any fact of actual intercourfe, unlefs what may arife from the vicinity of Mrs. Campbell's chamber and mine, a circumftance which if I repel, the probability of his teftimony can raife no reafonable fufpicion of guilt, efpecially as any other fituation in fmall ready-furnifhed lodgings is not to be had. This witnefs is produced principally for the purpofe of proving that I endeavoured to excite the paffions, and corrupt the morals of the lady, in order to complete my plan of feduction. With a view to eftablifh this, he fwears that I ordered him to buy fome fmutty prints, the moft fmutty prints he could find; that he did fo, and that he went into the room one day when I did not expect him: that I was looking at one of thofe prints, and Mrs. Campbell was looking over my fhoulder; that when he came in, fhe turned her head, and walked away towards the window.

The effect of this evidence, to ufe a common expreffion, was to run away with the court, the jury, and the audience, and to make an impreffion which was not removed while the trial lafted.

Pofitive

Positive and direct, however, as this testimony is, and strong as the impression may have been, I solemnly declare it to be false, and I shall proceed to shew, that upon deliberate consideration it must appear so to every candid and distinguishing mind.

In the first place, the object of this testimony as given, and the impression it made up on the Judge who tried the cause, was to support and perfect the plan of seduction. I ask them, if it can be supposed true, upon any principle of reason, that I should have found it necessary to have taken that means to seduce and excite a person to the practice of vice, in the month of June or July, 1789, when I had found, upon the supposition of familiarity at Ramsgate, such ready access to the object of my supposed desires, in the month of September, 1788, after an acquaintance of only three weeks duration, and an actual intercourse of two days? A case so contradictory deserves no credit, and the natural conclusion is, that both accounts are equally false.

But supposing that I had the design of inflaming the passions, and seducing the virtue of this young woman, by exhibitions of obscenity; is it probable that I should have desired a common servant
vant

vant to have been the purchaser of such a thing ? Even if I had been abandoned enough to have meant them for the private gratification of my own profligacy, it is a kind of secret I should have kept to myself, and therefore would have been myself the purchaser; and I should have been still more anxious to have concealed such a purchase, had I meant them for the secret purpose of corrupting another. Above all, I should scarcely have employed in that purchase, a servant who was quite new to me, who, according to his own testimony, had been but a few weeks in my service; and one whom I had thus employed, I should hardly have been improvident enough to have turned away in a few weeks after, without a character, and with every mark of displeasure and disapprobation, leaving it open to his malice and vindictiveness to expose me by a fact of so gross and vicious a nature.

That this person did buy prints for me I do not dispute, but it will appear from the fact of his having bought them, how completely incredible his story is. The prints I employed him to purchase were caricatures, to send to India for the amusement of my friends; and when he brought me the caricatures, he produced at the same time some such as he described, which I returned to him with difguft and reprehenfion, and ordered him to take them back, giving him money to pay for the caricatures only—the others remained unpaid ; and it appears from the affidavit of Mr. Whitehurft, with whom I lodged in Duke-ftreet, Manchefter-fquare,* fome time after, that the printfeller repeatedly called for payment, and that it was peremptorily refufed by me. Now, I afk whether it is confiftent with any rational fyftem of conduct, that I fhould not only have authorifed a public purchafe of fuch things, by a common fervant, after three weeks acquaintance with him, but that I fhould publicly, peremptorily, and re-peatedly refufe to pay the printfeller, and that at this moment they fhould remain unpaid, thereby leaving it open not only to the fabricator of this tale, but to the printfeller likewife, to eftablifh a fact of fuch a complexion againft me ? The wit-nefs ftates in his evidence, that he had the prints in court. Now, how could this be upon any other fuppofition than that which I have made, viz. that I returned them to him, when firft pro-duced to me by him ?

Is it to be fuppofed not only that I fhould have authorifed him to buy the prints, but that having

Appendix, p. 37, D. E. F.

been

been difcovered in exhibiting them, I fhould either then have given them back to him, or put it in his power to get them. The explanation is clear, he muft have retained the prints, notwith-ftanding my orders to reftore them ; the print-feller, therefore, not having received them, de-manded of me the money, and the witnefs re-taining them in his poffeffion, brought them out to confirm his teftimony. I cannot, therefore, for a moment doubt, whatever may have been the firft impreffion of difguft upon hearing this evidence, that when it is examined deliberately and difpaffionately, it will appear to be a wilful and fcandalous mifreprefentation.

The next witnefs called was Robert Green.* As he ftates a variety of facts and circumftances, tending to prove actual guilt, and eftablifhing the completion of my fuppofed plan of feduction, it is material to attend to his evidence moft mi-nutely.

He begins by faying that he came into my fervice when I refided in Duke-ftreet, Manchefter-fquare, 1790. The particular month of the year he does not mention ; that he had been in my fervice fix

* Appendix, p. 77, F.

weeks

weeks and a day or two, when he fays that he fufpected there was fomething improper *between an
uncle and a niece*; that he had the curiofity therefore to watch, and upon going into the drawing-
room one evening, faw us fitting on the couch,
*which ſtood behind the door, in a very criminal
way.* This is a fingular ſtile of expreſſion, and
not very like the language of a perfon in his ſta-
tion, nor at all fimilar to the general turn of expreſſion in the reſt of his evidence. It bears marks
of fuggeſtion from fome perfon of better education than the witnefs. But I would aſk, how
fhould he have feen us by going in at the door,
fitting on the couch behind the door ? If he could
fee any thing, it could only be by advancing into,
or towards the middle of the room. He then defcribes the pofition to be, my one arm around
Mrs. Campbell's neck, and the other under her
petticoats, and that he could plainly fee her naked knee. Now, examine this teſtimony by the
laws of probability.

First of all, it is not probable that upon his approach, we fhould have remained in any pofition
from which we could have withdrawn or reco-
vered ourfelves: becaufe it is not to be prefumed
that we meant to exhibit this to the view of the
fervant. This is not to be prefumed in any cafe,

but

but in this cafe it arifes out of the nature of the evidence that we wifhed to avoid difcovery, for according to his own ftory, he was obliged to watch his opportunity to difcover us.

He had a fufpicion, he fays, but not at firft ; after a time, he thought there was fomething improper going on between an uncle and niece ; and then, more from curiofity than any thing elfe, he went in the drawing-room.

Nature has implanted in the breaft of man an impulfe which leads him inftinctively to avoid difcovery in the connection between the fexes, even when it is moft innocent and irreprehenfible, fo that a difpofition to withdraw from any fituation which may indicate it, upon the rifk of being expofed to the view of others, is immediate. Surely this inftinctive difpofition is not diminifhed where the connection arifes from an unlawful intrigue, and is more particularly to be prefumed in fuch a cafe as the prefent. The prefumption therefore is, that on hearing a foot on the ftairs, ftill more on hearing the opening the door, we fhould have retired from the pofition we are defcribed to have been in—had it been practicable. Now, what is the pofition fixed on by the witnefs ? The gentleman's one hand in the

e   lady's

lady's bofom, and the other up her petticoats, fo
as to fhew her naked knee. The firft noife on
the ftairs, or movement of the door, would have
led him to withdraw his hands, and her to drop
her petticoats, an arrangement which could have
been performed in an inftant, replacing every
thing in a fituation to deftroy all appearance of
any thing *improper* or *criminal*. If an alteration
of a pofition, fuch as the witnefs defcribes, could
have been eafily accomplifhed on the firft noife,
it would have been accomplifhed to a certainty
before he could have advanced to any part of the
room, by which he could have feen the couch
behind the door, and the pofition of thofe who
were upon it. The witnefs, therefore, to have
preferved verifimilitude in his teftimony, fhould
have chofen fome pofition from which it would
have been more difficult for the parties to have
difembarraffed themfelves ; for as the teftimony
now ftands, it violates all the laws of probability,
and makes it natural to fift with fufpicion every
word this witnefs fays.

The witnefs then proceeds to tell a very mi-
nute ftory refpecting a quarrel between Mrs.
Campbell and myfelf; as follows :—" After this,
" that one day, Major Hook faid to Mrs. Campbell,
" I am going out now, and I will come in to
" dinner. I remember we had that day for din-

I   " ner

" ner a cod's head and founds, and Major Hook
" never came in to dinner. Mrs. Campbell
" waited very impatiently till six o'clock, when
" fhe feemed to be in a violent paffion, and or-
" dered me to take the dinner down, fhe fhould
" not eat any dinner. She feemed much enra-
" ged to think he did not come home to dinner;
" with that he came home, about half paft ten at
" night. When he came home, I let him in;
" he went up into the drawing-room, I went
" down into the kitchen. When I had been down
" there the courfe of a quarter of an hour, I
" heard a violent fcream, and a cry of murder;
" with that I went up ftairs into the drawing-
" room, and I perceived Major Hook ftanding in
" the corner of the room, with a chair before
" him, and fhe trying to ftrike him with a po-
" ker; with that he defired me to quit the room,
" which I did; I went down into the kitchen.
" I had not been there above five minutes, when
" I heard a violent crying out again, and Mrs.
" Campbell run down ftairs; this was about half
" paft eleven, or near twelve: fhe ran out into
" the ftreet, Major Hook followed her, and de-
" fired me to go after her, which I did; I fol-
" lowed her out, and I overtook her a little way
" down Duke-ftreet: fhe was in a deplorable
" condition, her handkerchief tore all off her

" neck,

" neck, and Major Hook with his waistcoat tore
" open, and down as far as here.* With that I
" said, says I, for God's sake Mrs. Campbell
" come in. Q. Did she come in ? A. I fol-
" lowed her, and overtook her, and said, Mrs.
" Campbell come in, consider what condition
" you are in, and the time of night, and you will
" be taken up by the watch, and put in the
" watch-house, with that she returned, and shut
" herself up in the parlour. Q. Did any thing
" else happen ? A. She shut herself up in the
" parlour, and Major Hook came and said, Har-
" riet, Harriet, I insist upon your coming out,
" *I pray you to come out* ; she came out, and was
" running up stairs, her foot slipp'd, and she fell
" down upon the landing-place, she fainted away,
" or pretended it, with that Major Hook stood
" over her, and proclaimed these words : ' You
' are a whore, a d—d whore, and the worst of
' whores.' She replied, I am a whore, but it is
' only to you, who ought to have been my fa-
' ther, my friend, and my protector ; instead of
' that, you have been my utter ruin, and my
' friends. Oh my poor husband !'

* Pointing to about three inches from the waist.

The

The cry, he fays, was a cry of murder, at a late hour in the evening, in a fmall houfe, where the landlord and the family lodged, as well as my family. I was heard from the drawing-room to the kitchen, and yet no perfon feems to have been alarmed but this witnefs; nay, it will appear from the affidavit of the landlord of the houfe, and his fervants, that they were in the houfe that very night, and were regularly in the houfe one or other of them every night, at that hour, and heard nothing of the cry of murder. Mrs. Campbell returned, as the witnefs fays, and went into the parlour, and that I begged and prayed her to come out, and go up ftairs, and that fhe fell upon the ftairs, and fainted away, or pretended to faint. Here again, I would defire the peculiar turn of expreffion and fet form of words to be remarked, and would afk if it is agreeable to probability that I fhould have taken the particular moment to proclaim the words fworn to. The fervant, according to his own account, was alarmed, and had gone out in queft of Mrs. Campbell, after the cry of murder; he was upon the watch, and to a certainty within my hearing, for no part of the houfe was out of it. Is it agreeable to probability, that I fhould have chofen to utter thofe expreffions the moment when fhe fainted, and that too upon the ftairs, where the words

fpoken

spoken 'muſt have been heard by all the family ?
And laſt of all, is it probable that ſhe ſhould have
made the obſervation ſworn to in the midſt of a
fit, into which he ſays ſhe had juſt fallen, or pretended to fall ? And is it not very inconſiſtent to
ſuppoſe, that I ſhould have been excited to ſuch
expreſſions by the event of her falling, or appear-
ing to fall in a fit, my temper of mind having
become ſo different (according to the teſtimony of the witneſs himſelf) from that of rage
or paſſion, or any diſpoſition of mind likely to
dictate opprobrious language; for he repreſents
me as coming to the parlour door, and in a
ſoothing manner, intreating her to come out ?

Mr. Whitehurſt ſays, in his affidavit,* that he
remembers the night on which Mrs. Campbell
went into the ſtreet, and was brought back by
Robert Green, when ſhe ſhut herſelf up in the
parlour, and ſhortly after went up to her bed-
room; that he did not on that evening, or at any
other period of time whatever, hear Mrs. Campbell cry our murder, or Major Hook ſay to Mrs.
Campbell, you are a ‘ whore, or a d—d whore,
‘ or the worſt of whores,’ or any other expreſſions
or words to the like purpoſe or effect. He ſays

* Appendix, p. 36, 37.

his

his niece Jones, and his fervant White, were in the houfe with him, and that his houfe is but a fmall one, that violent words fpoken in any part of it, muft be heard throughout the whole houfe.

Alice Jones, the niece,* fwears to the fame effect.

Elzabeth White,† the houfe maid, fays, fhe remembers the night that Mrs. Campbell went into the ftreet, and identifies it by the fame circumftances as Mr. Whitehurft, and Jones, and Green, viz. Green following her and bringing her back, and her going into the parlour. She then fays fhe came out to go up ftairs, *that fhe was with Mrs. Campbell upon the ftairs, and attended her up to bed*, and did not then, or at any other time, hear Major Hook ufe the expreffions mentioned by Green; and that they could not have been ufed at the time without her hearing them, becaufe fhe never was a moment abfent from her, from the time fhe fell in the fit, till the time fhe put her to bed—and the fame witnefs fwears that fhe did not hear the cry of murder.

* Appendix, p. 40,

† Appendix, p. 38, 39.

The

The evidence of Green, therefore, is not only improbable in itfelf, but it is directly contradicted by perfons who muft have heard what paffed, and by one in particular who fwears fhe was with Mrs. Campbell during the whole time, in which, by the teftimony of Green, the very extraordinary and difagreeable words were fpoken.

I beg leave now to confider before I go farther, who, and what is the character of this witnefs, and who are and what is the character of thofe who make the affidavits. The witnefs is a menial fervant, whom I turned off without a character, and who admits we parted in bad terms, who fays I *underminded* him, and hired another fervant before I let him know my intentions, and that he underftands I ufe all my fervants ill—a fingular charge againft a perfon fuppofed to be engaged in carrying on an inceftuous intrigue. Green therefore is a perfon upon whom motives of an indirect nature may be fuppofed to operate ; while the others are perfons of credit and reputation, whofe houfe I have long left, and who are liable to no prejudice, as they are under no obligation of any fort ; and thofe are the perfons who all fwear they never faw any improper conduct between Mrs. Campbell and myfelf : and Whitehurft fwears, that he would not have permitted

us

us to remain in his house if he had. It is likewise to be attended to, that these witnesses, particularly Whitehurst, swear that I took the
lodging for myself and my niece, and that her
mother and family came constantly to visit us.
These are circumstances which go a great way
to repel the presumption of an intrigue.

The witness next proceeds to state the appearance of Mrs. Campbell's bed in Duke-street, and
says he was shewn it by Betty White, the house-
maid of Mr. Whitehurst. The representation of
this matter rests upon his testimony alone, while
Betty White might have been produced to have
confirmed him. It is very material that such a
fact should not be left on the testimony of a single
witness, but should be confirmed. But if the
fact was to be left to the credit of one witness
only, two being equally in a situation to be produced; it must be evident that the person who
discovered and shewed the bed, must be the
most credible and satisfactory; but if that witness
is not called at all, but the witness who was
brought to see it, called, it must raise a strong
suspicion in the mind, that the original witness
would not have confirmed the testimony given.

The

The teſtimony of that witneſs, as well as of the others, appears in the affidavits, and ſhe gives a poſitive contradiction to this fact, ſaying that ſhe never called Robert Green into the bed-room, nor obſerved to him the mark of two people in the bed,* and that ſhe never ſaw any ſuch marks in the bed, nor had any ſuſpicion of them.

The witneſs then gives evidence reſpecting my conduct at Swanſea, particularly to his diſcovering Mrs. Campbell and myſelf in a moſt indecent ſituation in her bed-room. " Q. Do you remember " while at Swanſea going to a room adjoining " to her bed-room? A. I do, it was one day " after dinner; I was in the court-yard with " the children, and Major Hook's ſon ſaid I was " wanted; I went up ſtairs. Q. Did you go " into the room adjoining, where Major Hook " and Mrs. Campbell were? A. Yes, I went " into the room, and I perceived that Major " Hook and Mrs. Campbell were laying at the " foot of the bed. Q. Was it in her bed-room? " A. In her bed-room, and on her bed; as ſoon " as they ſaw me, it put them in a ſurprize, he " ſtarted up, and the flap of his breeches hung " down, and his face was as red as fire; the co-

* Appendix, p. 38, D.

" lour

" lour came all up in his face, and Mrs. Camp-
" bell walked to another part of the room. Q.
" At that time did you obferve any part of the
" perfon of Mrs. Campbell ? A. Yes, I did, I
" faw at that time up as far as here, *(pointing to*
" *her knee.)* Q. Her thighs ? A. Yes, I did.
" Q. Her naked thighs? A. Her naked thighs."
Green fays he only went into the children's room,
in which cafe it is impoffible he could have feen
the bed, as this plan fhewing the arrangement of
the rooms will prove.

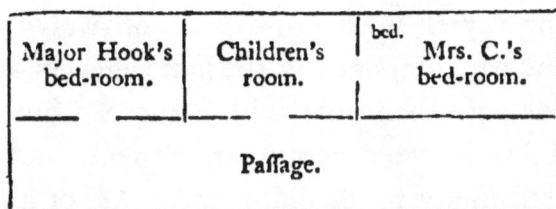

Major Hook's bed-room.	Children's room.	bed. Mrs. C.'s bed-room.
	Paffage.	

Now it is very fingular that a fervant fhould,
without ceremony, have thought himfelf intitled
to advance to the door of a lady's bed-chamber :
he therefore finds it neceffary to account for it by
faying my fon faid he was called. Now I muft
either have fent my fon for him, or the boy muft
have made a miftake, or the whole muft have
been a pretence : as to the firft, it is incredible
that I fhould have called him, in the fituation he
defcribed me to have been in ; as to the fecond,

it

it is not very likely that a boy of eleven or twelve years of age fhould, by miftake, defire that to be done for which he had no authority ; and if his pretence is falfified, it follows that but little credit is due to his fact.

It is to be obferved likewife, that all the rifks of difcovery are run without a fingle precaution upon any part. For the door is left unfecured, although the room adjoined that occupied by the children, who were then (as appears by his evidence) actually running about ; I was therefore expofing myfelf to be feen by a fon of twelve years old, and daughters nearly the fame age, in an inceftuous correfpondence with a niece. Surely it would require very confiftent, correct, and credible teftimony to eftablifh the belief of a ftory fo fingular and improbable.

In giving an account of the diftribution of rooms at Swanfea, he feems inclined to make an impreffion, as if the room in which I flept was adjoining to Mrs. Campbell's. Whereas the evidence of the next witnefs (his wife) makes it quite clear that the children's bed-room was between Mrs. Campbell's and mine, in the manner defcribed in the plan, and that there was no door into her bed-room but through that of the children ;

dren ; this he corrects by being re-examined, and
comes into the fame ftory with his wife ; but his
original evidence fhews a determined difpofition
to make fuch a ftory, and to eftablifh fuch ar-
rangements, as will lead to the fuppofition of intercourfe ; fuch a mifreprefentation, making his
bias manifeft and clear, muft lead to difcredit
every other part of his teftimony. In fome facts,
it is evident that he has fworn falfely, in others,
his pretences have been untrue ; in all, he has
violated probability. I do not go too far,
therefore, if I fay, that a witnefs who prevari-
cates in fome inftances, and tells an improbable
ftory in all, is to be believed in none.

Sarah Green,* the wife of this witnefs, was
next examined.

She eftablifhes it clearly as a fact, that at Swanfea, where we were fettled in family, Mrs.
Campbell's room was not next to mine, but that
the children's feparated them ; and that there was
no approach to her room, except through that of
the children's. But fhe fays, that upon the road
I was particular in having the bed-rooms together ; and that I ordered two rooms only, I and

* Appendix, p. 83, F.

2 my

my fon flept in one, a fingle beded room, and Mrs. Campbell and my girls in a double room. She fays that at the next inn to Swanfea, we would not take the rooms if they were not adjoining, if we travelled all night, and this fact is refted on as a proof of our guilty connection; while, inftead of founding a prefumption of guilt, I confidently afk whether thefe facts do not eftablifh the ftrongeft prefumption of innocence; and whether taking the whole of this part of the evidence together, it does not prove that the motive of this arrangement was not a guilty intercourfe, but was that of giving protection to an apprehenfive perfon? In the firft place, it is evident that I was travelling publicly with my whole family, with fervants attending my niece, myfelf, and my children, and not clandeftinely for the purpofe of an intrigue. The orders for the bed-rooms were openly given, and when the accommodations we required were not to be had, it feems we preferred travelling on to remaining. If the object had been guilty enjoyment, there could be no motive for continuing to travel, for that prevented its completion as effectually, as if the rooms had been a-part; therefore no rational ground can be given for my conduct, but the fears which many females are liable to in fleeping at an inn, without any perfon whom

they

they have confidence in near them to protect
them.

Some stress is laid, however, on her ordering
her door, and that of the children's room, to be
left open, at Swanfea, when no other inference
can be drawn with fairnefs, than that fhe might,
by that means, have it in her power to have
communication with the children, for it did not
preferve the communications between my room
and her's.

There is one circumftance, however, mentioned by this witnefs, on which fhe feems to
reft fome proof of guilt, viz. that at night I
fhould have come frequently into Mrs. Cambell's
room, half undreffed, when Mrs. Campbell was
undreffed ; this fhe accompanies with an obfervation, that on thofe occafions I immediately retired
when I faw her. Now if all the circumftances
are fairly weighed, it is apparent that my motive
for withdrawing could not be a confcioufnefs of
guilt, but muft have arifen from my perceiving
Mrs. Campbell's fituation : and it will not be
fuppofed, I truft, in the habits of domeftic intercourfe, that the father and mafter of a family
muft have impure intentions, becaufe he is feen
going about his houfe in undrefs, a fituation very
                                                    diftinct

diſtinct from nakedneſs. Had my object then been a guilty intercourſe with Mrs. Campbell, I ſhould have probably been cautious not to have expoſed myſelf a ſecond time to Mrs. Green ; and the having been ſeen repeatedly in that ſituation, is in itſelf a ſtrong preſumption of innocence of mind. But if not in itſelf a proof of innocence of mind, is it to be taken as evidence of open intercourſe and frequent guilt ?—Open intercourſe and frequent guilt muſt have been attended with great facility in proving numerous inſtances of intercourſe, or very evident marks of it. Now, the evidence of any thing like intercourſe at Swanſea, is confined to the ſingle and extraordinary caſe ſworn to by Green, and repreſented to have taken place in the afternoon in a room with an open door, when all the family were ſtirring about, and the children running to and fro at play. And as to the marks and appearance of frequent intercourſe, Mrs. Green, who was examined very minutely as to the bed, declares ſhe obſerved nothing particular ; no appearance of two people having been in it at any time. Had my object been to have gone to bed to Mrs. Campbell, when I was ſeen in undreſs by Mrs. Green, going into Mrs. Campbell's bed-room, it is impoſſible that the ſame witneſs, who ſays ſhe always made the beds, ſhould not have perceived

the

the condition of the bed, if it had betrayed any
marks of intercourse ; and it is very unlikely that
if there had been any thing of this kind to difcover, that Green, who states the condition of
the bed from Betty White, should not have
stated the same facts from the information of his
own wife, with whom the delicate scruple of not
pointing out particular marks need not have
prevented his evidence from being perfect ; a de-
fect, which, upon his crofs-examination, his
evidence seems to labour under respecting the bed
in Duke-street.

Besides, the fact of my going to Mrs. Campbell's room with a criminal view, in the manner,
and with the frequency described, establishes a
presumption of such frequent intercourse, as must
have led to easy detection. How comes it then
that Green, the husband, who avows his early
curiosity—who swears he watched us in the
drawing-room, in Duke-street—who swears he
came without ceremony into Mrs. Campbell's bed-
room at Swansea, should have been unable, notwithstanding this supposed openness of intercourse, to have discovered, either at the inns on
the road, at Swansea, or elsewhere, any more
decisive fact of criminal intercourse, than the
indecent but impossible discovery in the drawing-

g   room

room in Duke-ftreet, and the equally improbable one in the bed-room at Swanfea ? For this
reafon, that my intercourfe with Mrs. Campbell was of the pureft nature, that it was (in
the abfence of parents) the intercourfe of a pro-
tecting father, with an innocent and forfaken
child, and upon that principle, all appearances of
familiarity, which in another connection might
afford a prefumption of guilt, are to be explained
and accounted for.

Elizabeth Hearne,* the next witnefs, fet out
with fwearing that I lived at Mrs. Frafer's in
Brook-ftreet, a good while ; the fact is, as appears from the affidavits, that I never lived
there at all.—At Walton again fhe fays, I came
occafionally ; whereas there Mrs. Frafer and her
children, and I and my children, lived together
in family.

This woman fays that fhe watched, from a
curiofity raifed by having heard me go into the
room before ; and that fhe made the bed in the
morning, and it appeared *as if more than one
had flept in it.* The precife form of expreffion
in this cafe is fingular, and not free from fufpi-

* Appendix, p. 88, A.

cion :

cion : but the teftimony is moft extraordinary, indeed, when confidered under all its circum- ftances; fhe fays it was in November, 1788, that fhe faw this, but is not fure as to the month; but fhe is fure that there was nobody in the houfe but the gardener and his family; and my fervant; that Mrs. Frafer was not at Walton. In fact, the houfe at Walton was not taken till the end of December, 1788, and Mrs. Campbell and myfelf had gone there to give directions about the houfe. There could therefore be no opportunity to excite that curiofity which led her to watch; and as to the opportunity of feeing us any where elfe, it is out of the queftion, for I never did live in Brook-ftreet, nor under the fame roof with Mrs. Campbell, until her mother, Mrs. Frafer's family, and mine, united at Walton.

The fame witnefs fwears to Captain Campbell having been at Walton; when it will appear by his own letters, that he never was there, nor ever faw his wife, from the month of December, 1788, although he did not fail from Torbay till March, 1789. This circumftance may give fome idea of the veracity and accuracy of the witnefs.

The

The conduct of the next witnefs, Andrew
Addifon, when he was brought to be fworn, will
fhew the complexion of the teftimony produced
againft me.

   " Andrew Addifon called,* the oath being ten-
" dered, he was obferved not to kifs the book,
" upon which Lord Kenyon faid, adminifter the
" oath to him again, what is the meaning he
" will not kifs the book ? The oath was re-ad-
" miniftered. *Lord Chief Juftice.* Now kifs
" the book. The witnefs then kiffed the book,
" and faid, I never was in a court before to give
" evidence. Mr. *Mingay.* Now you are upon
" your oath, had you any intention to avoid kif-
" fing the book upon your oath ? A. Upon my
" oath I had not. *Lord Chief Juftice.* If I was
" upon oath, I fhould fay I believe he had. Mr.
" *Erfkine.* Then I certainly will not call a
" witnefs that my Lord makes fuch an obferva-
" vation upon."†

Arabella

   * Appendix, p. 92, C.

   † JAMES WALKER, fervant to William Paxton,
Efq. of Queen-fquare, Bloomfbury, in the county
of Middlefex, maketh oath and faith, that he knows Andrew Addifon, and that on Monday the 25th day of February, 1793, he, this deponent attended the court of
King's Bench, Weftminfter, to give evidence in a caufe
depend-

Arabella Kennedy,* speaks to nothing that can give occasion to discussion, as she establishes no

depending between Major Archibald Hook, and Captain Charles Collins Campbell, for criminal conversation with Mrs. Harriet Campbell, wife to the said Captain Charles Collins Campbell, and which was expected to have come on that day, but for reasons unknown to this deponent, was deferred till the Tuesday following : And he, this deponent, further saith, that on the said 25th day of February, 1793, he met the said Andrew Addison in the lobby near the House of Commons, and conversed with him, the said Andrew Addison, on a variety of subjects, among which the then depending trial was one, whereupon the said Andrew Addison told him, this deponent, in the hearing of John Lewin, servant to the said Major Archibald Hook, that he the said Addison would give his evidence in court, but would not kiss the book.

JAMES WALKER.

Sworn in London this 15th Day of March, 1793, before Hugh Cleghorn, Esq. one of his Majesty's Justices of the Peace for the County of Middlesex.

HUGH CLEGHORN.

JOHN LEWIN, servant to Major Archibald Hook, maketh oath and saith, that he knows Andrew Addison, and that on Monday the 25th day of February, 1793, he, this deponent, accompanied James Walker, servant to William Paxton, Esq. down to the court of King's

* Appendix, p. 92, F.

I   Bench

no fact that can be perverted into a fufpicion of guilt.

As to Woodroff,* the gardener's evidence, he eftablifhes nothing but that I was in the paffage, not fully dreffed, a circumftance to which it will be ftrange to attach criminality. He, however, afcertains the time of our being at Walton, and the purpofe to have been to fix the houfe for Mrs. Frafer, and in fo doing, he renders the teftimony of Elizabeth Hearne incredible, on the ground ftated in the anfwer to her teftimony.

Bench, Weftminfter, and that near the Houfe of Commons they, the faid James Walker and this deponent, met the faid Andrew Addifon : And he this deponent further faith, that the faid Andrew Addifon told James Walker, in his, this deponent's hearing, that he the faid Addifon would give his evidence in court, but would not kifs the book ; whereupon he this deponent obferved to him, the faid Addifon, that if he did not kifs the book, his evidence would not be taken.

JOHN LEWIN.

Sworn at London this 15th of March, 1793, before Hugh Cleghorn, Efq. one of his Majefty's Juftices of the Peace for the County of Middlefex.

HUGH CLEGHORN.

* Appendix, p. 94, F.

It

It may not be improper to remark, that all this clafs of witneffes, who fpeak the conduct at Walton, fpeak of a period antecedent to the fuppofed difplay of the prints; and in that refpect, contradict the cafe as founded upon the ground of feduction; for it is abfurd to fuppofe that I fhould have attained my ends in December, 1788, and that I fhould yet have been attempting to feduce in June 1789.

The evidence of Jane Grimes* of the fituation at Bourne is, indeed, of a moft fingular nature. The looking through the key-hole of my bed-room door, on fufpicion, created by no motive that appears, but becaufe accident had led her up ftairs to receive orders from Mrs. Campbell for the grocer. The feeing me laying ftark naked, with my face downward, and Mrs. Campbell fitting by, full dreffed, a pofition fo abfurd, that the witnefs herfelf thinks it neceffary to account for it by fuppofing I had come from bathing. Mrs. Campbell's drawing the curtain, and thereby preventing more to be feen, is altogether fuch a tale as would require fome better teftimony than

* Appendix, p. 96, H.

that

that of a common liar, (which this woman is,) to make it obtain the smallest credit.*

It is most singular, that if such was our inter-course, we should never have been discovered but in this one instance, by this prying and suspicious woman. I lived at East Bourne, in a very small lodging, with a large family, consisting of Mrs. Campbell, a young lady of sixteen years old (Miss Hay) who constantly slept in the room with Mrs. Campbell, three children, and all the servants. Nothing improper could take place without a discovery, and Miss Hay's affidavit† will shew how little ground there is for suspicion; therefore, the only story that this woman could contrive, was one such as this, in which she could not be contradicted by any witness, however at variance with probability. What must strike as equally singular is, that this woman lived with me as cook at Ham. If the connection prevailed at all, it prevailed then, and yet, instead of fixing on any act of intercourse there, she confines her evidence to that single and extraordinary position seen through the key hole at

* Witnesses were in court to prove her character as a liar.

† Appendix, p. 46, 47.

East

Eaft Bourne, and obftructed by the drawing of a curtain, when there could be no reafon for drawing it, becaufe nobody was fufpected of obferving.

Mifs Macaulay,* the laft witnefs called, fpea's pofitively to the correct behaviour of Mrs. Campbell, and there the evidence ends—Evidence which, with the exception of Sarah Green, Arabella Kennedy, and Mifs Macaulay, I have no hefitation in branding with every epithet which confcious innocence can apply to deliberate guilt.

I am aware of the rifk that attends this charge; but I boldly make it, being determined to trace and bring to juftice thofe who have contrived the plot by which I fuffer; a plot palpable, as I contend, from the obfervations I have made on the teftimony of the witneffes, but rendered ftill more clear and decifive, by the *extrajudicial* conduct of the parties.

In the BON TON MAGAZINE,† publifhed for the month of February 1793, there is an additional

* Appendix, p. 99, F.
† Appendix, p. 109.

h   leaf

leaf annexed to the number, entitled, " *A fin-* " *gular* Account of the Trial of Major Hook for " Criminal Converfation with his Niece, Mrs. ".Campbell, tried before Lord Kenyon on the " 26th of February." After this title, and be- fore proceeding to give an account of the trial, which is given in a moſt unfair and partial man- ner, there is the following entry or notandum :

" See the plate entitled " *The Marrow-bone* " *Uncle, &c.* and for a tête-a-tête of the par- " ties turn to the firſt article of this number, " which was *printed off before* the event of this " trial was known."

The ſcandalous and beaſtly indecency of the plate is ſhocking to the laſt degree : but as it ap- plies to this cauſe, it is moſt important to denote the malicious mind which has been at work againſt me : the plate or engraving is meant to reprefent Mrs. Campbell and myſelf, and it aims at being a caricature of my face and perſon. Now is it poſſible that this could have been ac- compliſhed without the aid and communication of my profecutors ? How were the ordinary pub- liſhers of a magazine, or thoſe employed by them, to obtain any traces of a perſon, a ſtranger to England, not known in public life, very ſeldom

I   in

in London fince 1789, and living in retirement
with a narrow circle of friends, unlefs I had been
pointed out by thofe who knew me; through the
means of this caufe. The fuggeftion is confirmed by the other part of the publication. It
appears tha the *téte-a-téte* was printed off before
the event of the trial was known, contains a ftory
refembling that brought into court, defcribing
the connection and the country of all, and giving
the names of fome of the parties, and mentioning
feveral facts and circumftances which belong to
this caufe. Now how could thofe matters come
to the knowledge of the author of the magazine,
fo as to be printed off before the trial of the
caufe had taken place, unlefs they had been
privately communicated, as I have already ftated?
I am a retired individual, little known in England, Mrs. Campbell equally unknown. The
mere bringing of the action could difclofe none
of the facts or circumftances, becaufe the record,
as every body knows, gives no information, but
ftates merely the nature of the injury in formal
words.

The connection between the parties tending
to aggravate the crime, could, therefore, be
known to thofe only, who were acquainted with

the

the private circumftances of the caufe.* It is
evident, therefore, that there was an unjuft, ma-
lignant fpirit, fecretly at work, fupplying prints
and ftories for a magazine, in a matter not within the fcope of the knowledge of the authors of
fuch a work ; and, therefore, directly imputa-
ble to the actors in this wicked confpiracy to
ruin my peace, and tending ftrongly to manifeft
the difpofition of the parties to procure proof in
court to fupport that cafe which they fabricated
by anticipation for a periodical publication.

In addition to the other proofs annexed to this
cafe, I have added an affidavit of innocence made
by Mrs. Campbell, and I have added affidavits
and letters in fupport of her character and my
own,† by thofe who have long known us, and
have lately lived in intimacy with both : I have
likewife annexed the letters of Captain Campbell to her and to me, and letters from his father

* This extraordinary production concludes with an
addrefs to the fathers, brothers, and uncles, who may be
jurymen in the caufe, calling upon them to give exem-
plary damages. A feature denoting ftrongly the motive
which actuated the publifher in this cafe, and making it
clear that the publication is not fupplied in the regular
courfe of magazine intelligence.—See the end of the Trial.
† Appendix, p. 50, 51, 52, 53.

to

to me at the time I went to Scotland with Mrs. Campbell in 1788.

From thefe documents the public and my friends will be enabled to form a judgement of the charaÊers of the different parties, and from thence to conclude refpeÊing the probability of the truth of this cafe, and to decide between the alternative of aÊual guilt, or falfe charge.

Under the afflicting calamity of this verdiÊ, it is a folace to me to find that my charaÊer is ftill fuftained by the refpeÊable perfons who have made the affidavits and written the letters annexed.

The letters of Captain Campbell are given at large in this appendix, and they contain much matter for obfervation and difcuffion. I fhall only obferve here, however, that they eftablifh this faÊ, that from the commencement of his marriage, Captain Campbell and his wife lived without interruption in a ftate of domeftic mi-fery; a faÊ of importance to my cafe, becaufe when contrafted with the pofitive teftimony of his brothers and his fifter-in-law,* who fwear,

* Appendix, p. 1, to 24.

to

to their unvaried domeftic happinefs, it fhews the latitude they had given themfelves, eftablifhes what I have repeatedly remarked, the ftrong bias of the evidence in favour of the plaintiff, without regard to truth, and manifefts the determination of the plaintiff in contradiction to his own letters, and in fpite of his confcioufnefs to the contrary, to affert and endeavour to prove whatever he thought would benefit his caufe.

This fact is of equal importance in another view, by eftablifhing a prefumption, at leaft, that no traces of affection or family delicacy would ftand in the way of his ufing every mean to accomplifh a fcheme which might tend either to the gratification of his caprice, his avarice, or his malignity. Captain Campbell writes in one letter that they were miferable from the beginning of their marriage ; in another, that he never could feel a moment's peace till feas and feas divided them, and that he will never write to her again ; and in a third, that all the world faw their mifunderftanding, that he had come to a determination to keep a miftrefs. This refolution to feparate from Mrs. Campbell runs through the whole, and it appears that he had
even

even ordered the deed of feparation to be made
out.

His capricious difpofition is manifeft in every
line, and it is difficult to decide whether the bad-
nefs of his temper or his heart, is moft likely to
have dictated his conduct. The letters of his
father,* which in my own vindication and that
of Mrs. Campbell I am forced to make public,
and which nothing but this perfecution could
have wrung from my moft fecret repofitories—
difplay an aged and afflicted father, lamenting
over the vices of a profligate fon. Such tefti-
monies from fuch a quarter authorize me to af-
firm, that the motives which I have afcribed to
the plaintiff are the real motives which dictated
his proceedings againft me, and confirm what is
fworn to in fome of the affidavits refpecting the
undue means taken to obtain the teftimony which
was produced againft me.† Upon the whole,
when it is confidered that the cafe of feduction
opened and refted upon as the ground of my
guilt, was contradicted in the very firft ftage of
the proof by evidence, which, in place of feduction, eftablifhed a fact of flagrant proftitution in

* Appendix, p. 24 to 32.
† Appendix, p. 34, G. D. and p. 45, E. A.

the

the fuppofed fcene at Ramfgate. When it is confidered that my taking Mrs. Campbell to Scotland was fuggefted by Captain Campbell himfelf, and never propofed or hinted at by me. That on that journey no familiarity is alledged, nor any trace of evidence given of it, although Captain Campbell followed us almoft immediately from ftage to ftage, and his *agents* have fince traced us in our route.

When it is confidered that the laws of probability, thofe fure, unerring, and eftablifhed rules by which to try the credibility of all human teftimony, are violated in every part of the evidence given by the witneffes; and that the teftimony of the witneffes, efpecially that of Robert Green, is contradicted pofitively in its moft effential parts by affidavits in which the facts fworn to, coincide with and are fupported by the nature of the tranfactions, and the circumftances in which they took place.—When it is confidered that Mrs. Campbell has now for nearly five years lived in my houfe, and under my protection, and that in all that period four inftances only of guilty intercourfe or indecent fituation are fpecified by the witneffes, although thofe fituations, and the whole tenor of our conduct, according to the teftimony of the fame witneffes, reprefent us

as

as the moſt unguarded and inconſiderate of human creatures, and although the witneſſes repreſent themſelves as excited by the ſtrongeſt curioſity to diſcover our connection.—When it is conſidered that diſintereſted witneſſes ſwear to the propriety of our mutual behaviour, and that there is the ſtrongeſt teſtimony to character that can be given.—When it is conſidered that the black and ſuſpicious character of the plaintiff is derived from ſources which cannot err, (the evidence of his father's letters and his own) and that attempts upon witneſſes have been traced, ſpecified, and ſworn to.—When all theſe things are conſidered, I ſubmit to my friends and the public, with anxiety, but with confidence, that I have completely eſtabliſhed my innocence. It ſhall be the unremitting object of my life, to confirm the belief of that innocence beyond the poſſibility of doubt, by diſcovering the means of obtaining juſtice againſt thoſe whoſe crimes have brought upon me this unforeſeen and dreadful misfortune. To ſecure ſucceſs to this great and important object, I was told that in prudence I ſhould poſtpone the preſent publication.: in compliance with this ſuggeſtion I deliberated, but found the continuance of ſuch an exertion totally deſtructive of my peace of mind.

i   APPEN-

that others in the strongest testimony to character that can be given.—When it is considered that the black and suspicious character
of the plaintiff is derived from sources which
notice have been traced, specified, and shewn to—
When all these things are considered, I submit
to my friends and the public, with anxiety, but
with confidence, that I have completely esta-
blished my innocence." It shall be the continuing object of my life, to confirm the belief of
by discovering the means of obtaining justice
against those whose crimes have brought upon

APPENDIX.

No. I.

Captain Campbell to his Wife.

London, Feb. 15, 1788.

DEAR HARRIET,

I AM at a lofs how to write, accufed of every thing A
that is bad, and every thing to make a woman miferable, &c. I never fhall forget *what has paffed* between your mother and me; to her I folely impute all
my misfortunes—all I have *fuffered,* and all that I have
yet to *fuffer;* and although I never will fhew her my B
feelings, I never can be at a moment's eafe in her
company. This, Harriet, is your mother I am talk-
ing of, &c.

I have made up my mind to go to India, but,
Harriet, you fhall not go with me. C

I was not a week married when your mother faid to
me *what would ftamp any, and every, man's mifery in
the marriage ftate,* &c.

I am going to a country that is expenfive, and fhall D
have enough to do to keep myfelf, &c.

(Signed) C. C.

A

No.

No. II.

Captain Campbell to his Wife.

Monday Evening, March 31, 1788.

A   I HAVE obferved for fome time paft, that your fifter's governefs, inftead of knowing her diftance, has made herfelf more familiar (than I chofe to be witnefs to) with you. I obferved her more than once go into your room, &c.

B   It was always your *way* to keep low company. It is not long fince *fervants* were your intimates. You are adopting the *mode Mrs. McNiel began*—firft the governefs, then the governor, *till it arrived at the moft menial fervant in the houfe.* Do you think that I can

C return to you with any degree of fatisfaction, after knowing your *affociates?*

(Signed)   C. C.

No. III.

Captain Campbell to his Wife.

Chatham, July 18, 1788.

D   I HAVE ferioufly reflected on your going to India with me, but for various reafons I wifh to propofe your remaining at home the firft feafon, and I wifh you to confult your friends upon the fubject, before you make any reply. I really am of opinion it will be conducive to both our happinefs and my intereft, which, in

E the end, you will find the *benefit* of. I hope you will have my intereft fufficiently at heart to give up all thoughts of going at prefent. I hope you will ferioufly weigh this matter: I, myfelf, am decidedly of opinion to remain at home, in preference to your going out with me.

Your's affectionately,

(Signed)   C. C.

No.

No. IV.

Captain Campbell to his Wife.

Auguſt 24, 1788.

I HAVE received your letter from Ramſgate of **A**
the 20th, and am much obliged by your ſending the
muſic I aſked for a fortnight ago. The idea of your
intended excurſion to Ramſgate, I ſuppoſe occupied
your mind ſo much, that you had not time to give
yourſelf the trouble of ſpeaking about it : *if I wait for
it till you ſee me, I aſſure you I never will have it.* But
I did not depend on you for it, for I have already wrote **B**
to Miſs Macaulay to get it ſent to me, &c.

*Do not oblige me to repeát ſo often that we never meet
again on any account whatever. It is aſtoniſhing to me that
you have* FOR THREE YEARS TOGETHER *acted in direct
oppoſition to every thing I could wiſh.* It is evident you
prefer living with a mother, and you are perfectly
right ; at the ſame time I ſhould expoſe myſelf as a
fool, were I to allow you to come to me again, &c. **C**
I ſay you are not *true* ; no, *never can I feel a moment's
peace, till ſeas and ſeas divide us.*

I ſhall go up to London and take away every article
I have in that *curſed houſe* I once lived in ; and *remember you may feel before many years are over your head,*
the *juſt* recompence for your *conduct* As I hope to **D**
be ſaved I never will write you again.

(Signed)   C. C,

No. V.

Captain Campbell to his Wife.

E

(Extracts.)   *Hilſea, 19th Sept.* 1788.

" YOU ſhew your mother your diſlike to me ; ſhe
" told me you ſaid you never could like me as a huſ-

"band: you deny it, but in all your actions you shew
"it. *The whole world see there is a misunderstanding*
"*between us*, and they believe it. I am asked why I
"do not bring you with me; would you have me say
"you will not come? Must I expose my foolish sub-
A "mission, &c.

: "I hope you have been happy at your bathing; it
"has been *dear bathing* to me, *it ought to be of service*
"*to you.* Is the water of Ramsgate better than else-
"where? Your mother ought to have told you, you
;" had a husband, and to have thought of him instead
"of Mrs. Barclay—but I mean to write to your mother
B "as soon as I have settled my affairs, for which purpose
"I am going to London, &c."

Again, 20*th*.—"It is your decided choice and wish
"of being away from me that hurts me, and not your
"absence itself.—*I had once determined publicly to have*
"*taken a mistress*, &c, &c."
C "Notwithstanding the distance, I should not have
"thought of the expence had you ever in your life
"told me you wished to see me; but I perceive, Har-
"riet, that absence is the only means of making us
"happy, &c. &c. &c.
"If you have any thing to say to me don't wait my
"writing as I have plenty to occupy my pen.
(Signed) C. C.

D N. B. All these letters are previous to my journey
to Ramsgate, and most of them prior to my return to
England.

No. VI.

Captain Campbell to his Wife.

E *Pool's Coffee-House,*
Edinburgh, Oct. 25, 1788.
IT is now too late to say any thing on the *subject*,
but I can never have an opinion of you: I am confi-
dent

dent you will stick at nothing to *gratify* yourself. I have told every body, that I knew nothing of your plans, and am come in *pursuit* of you to know your reasons, and why you avoided me. I have submitted long enough, and you have now brought matters to a public crisis, and a little time will put it out of your power to distract me more, &c. I am now perfectly calm and decided in my future conduct towards you; not that I tell you this to make you uneasy, for your heart is as hard as a stone, and long as it has troubled me, self-preservation requires that I should think no longer of you. Your uncle has been the cause, though, indeed, you only wanted an opportunity to shew yourself; *and your uncle, of whom I had a good opinion, may now be sorry all his life-time that he has been the innocent cause of my everlasting wretchedness.* While I am in Scotland, I will arrange my affairs, &c. &c. As soon as your uncle arrives in London, I will take the liberty of desiring him to meet me, when our *separation* shall be settled, without disturbance or argument between us, all of which I wish to avoid, as perfectly useless and unnecessary. I inclose you a copy of my letter to your uncle, which is all till he leaves Campbell-town. As your uncle has a fortune, it will enable him to be of *service* to you: I hope he will act *liberally*, which I intend to recommend to him; you can surely expect nothing from me, &c.

(Signed) C. C.

—————

No. VII.

Captain Campbell to his Wife.

Campy, near Edinburgh,
Saturday Morning.

THAT cursed girl P—y M'D—d. I warned you before marriage, I warned you since, and you know I felt my bed prostituted by her having slept with my
love.

love. Make ever happy by affuring me you will ever renounce *P—y M'D—d*. Drop *her* for ever. Ever fince I have known her, which was before you faw her, fhe was *flightly* talked of; my honour is at ftake,

A &c. &c.

Again.—My fifter tells me you afked her to go to Campbell-town with you, but her anfwer was, " that " fhe could not, as it might not be agreeable to her " hufband." Even a father, who was always moft indulgent to her, did not make her forget the duty of

B a wife, even to that hufband who you know is fcarcely *more than a brute*, &c. &c.

Again—I muft refume the fubject of *P—y.* You know fhe muft be *notorious* before you knew it, &c. I told you of *Mifs Weft*, &c. &c.

I fhall know by your anfwer to my queftion whe-

C ther you are deceitful. I faw your letter and the contents; it was lively, and every thing I could wifh, but touched an *improper fubject.* Never, never fhall my feelings be the fame. Am I your Charles? Yes! And who is *your Blair*, that you write to P—y about,

D and where is he? I know you have entered into her *love affairs*, &c. &c.*

(Signed) C. C.

* To explain the foregoing, it is nececeffary to mention that

E Mifs Mary M'Donald, at the defire of her intimate friend and companion (Mrs. Campbell) had fent her picture in profile, which was brought as far as London by one gentleman ; and as Mrs. Campbell was then in France with her mother, it was given to another gentleman who was going to France (one Blair) and who engaged to deliver it; but from unforefeen circumftances, he never went to the place where fhe was, nor has fhe ever in her life-time

F feen him. In all her letters to her amiable friends, fhe expreffes her anxiety for the picture; fometimes faying, where is Mr. Blair? where is he gone? and in one, where is my Blair? alluding to the picture which he had for her, and in the letter which Captain Campbell faw to Mifs P—y M'D——d. " I hear *my Blair* is " now in London; I fhall at laft get my dear Mary,"—meaning the picture.

No.

(7)

No. VIII.

Captain Campbell to his Wife.

Inverary, Tuesday, Nov. 4th, 1788.

I AM just arrived here with my sister and Betsey; I could have sworn I should have found you here. Harriet, you have deceived me from the beginning of this business; nothing but your fixed resolution of being but *two* days in Kintyre induced me to submit to have an assent extorted from me, which, after expressing my feelings, &c. I was much hurt to find you so ready to grasp at. Neither my time nor my sister's will admit of my proceeding to Kintyre; indeed, I never had a thought of it when I set out from Edinburgh; but had I had the least idea of your *notions or plans,* or had I not thought you had determined to adhere to your *promise* to me of staying but two days, I could with ease have overtaken you at Dunbarton, before you set off on Sunday morning. I must now desire that you will immediately, on receipt of this, leave Kintyre: you have been imprudent to travel by day, and *too late at night* to fly from me. I must expect you will do the same to come to me. Whatever your plans are, I desire they may by no means prevent your leaving Campbell-town, or wherever you may be, on receipt of this, which will be on Friday the 7th instant, and I expect you will travel to be here on Saturday. I will ride on Saturday as far as Lochgilp-head, which is twenty miles from this; but I must return the same day here, as I repeat, neither my time nor my sister's will admit of longer delay. I cannot suppose Mrs. Campbell of Saddle has any ways detained you; it will be but a lame excuse, indeed, to have sacrificed the *feelings* of a husband a *second time* for the gratification of any living soul. You have

I   *judged*

judged for me and my feelings in this affair—I *will* for
A you in going to India. Write me alfo by Friday's
poft to Inverary.

(Signed) C. C.

No. IX.

Captain Campbell to his Wife.

(Extract.)   *Tuefday Evening*, 1788.

B I WROTE you this morning.
" You have acted *deceitful* and *bafe*. I wrote you
" from Edinburgh, which you would receive laft Fri-
" day, and did!—But after your promife of two days,
C " &c.—*What you did fince*, I muft keep to myfelf,
" but you have acted *brutally* to a hufband:—but you
" may feel the weight of my refentment," &c. &c. &c.
Running on in the fame ftile for upwards of twenty
pages.

(Signed) C. C.

No. X.

Captain Campbell to his Wife.

Wednefday Night, *Tarbot*.

D I AM juft arrived here, and fhall fleep at White-
houfe, and to-morow morning fhall proceed to Saddle,
there being a good road that way. On receipt of this,
I defire you will immediately fet off for Saddle, as I
E fhall wait there till you arrive: but I muft infift on
your coming alone, as I want to fpeak to you; and if
          a *living*

a *living soul* comes with you, I shall set off for Invera- A
ry, without waiting an hour in Kintyre. I wrote you
a letter yesterday from Inverary, which you will receive the same time as this.

(Signed)   C. C.

No. XI.

Captain Campbell to his Wife.

*White-house, Wednesday Night,
Eight o'Clock.*

YOU have drove me to despair. Is this your pro- B
mise of staying only two days with a man living in adultery—a bastard child and a whore in his house !* I
would most willingly have resigned my commission, in
preference to your being in Scotland with your uncle.
Where is your pride, your honour, to sacrifice a hus- C
band for an uncle of three week's acquaintance? He
shall know the weight of my resentment. I shall set off
for Saddle to-morrow at seven o'clock. God send
you strength of mind to bear what you will have to see—
but, by G—d, I am determined. I desire you will D
rise early, and set out to meet me in a carriage. I
cannot come on this night, for neither my horse, the
agitation of my mind, nor fatigue I have undergone,
will admit it. I desire you may be by yourself, for if
there is a single person with you, by the eternal God I E
will ride back as soon as I see you : be collected, for
I am resolved on explaining every thing, and having
an explanation before we *separate.* You have acted
deceitful and base—unworthy my attention. I have

* The person here meant is his father, Col. C. Campbell.

B

wrote

wrote Major Hook of what he may expect,* but I have taken the neceffary precaution of not inclofing it to you.

(Signed) C. C.

———————

No. XII.

Captain Campbell to his Wife.

Hilfea, Dec. 9th, 1788.

MY DEAREST FRIEND,

A   I RECEIVED a letter from Major Hook, your uncle, with one inclofed from my father. I had already made up my mind on this fubject, becaufe I was urged to it by the ftile of your conduct to me fince I left Saddle, &c.

B   I bear no refentment—God forbid I fhould towards you. I will write no more on this fubject, till you have fully converfed with, and confulted with your friend. Be fo good as to afk the papers of feparation to be made out by a ftranger, for I have yet feel-

C   ing left: fign them and fend them to me to be figned. When time has operated the change, we can deftroy the papers, and in the deftruction of them we may feel the greater pleafure. Let it be fecret that fuch papers exift, if you pleafe, but this I leave to you. I will

D   moft cheerfully correfpond with you, if agreeable; but by this meafure neither of us have a right to find fault

* See letter alluded to, No. XVIII. from Captain Campbell to Major Hook.

with

with one another's conduct, while feparate. I requeft
that you will let your uncle know of my anfwer and re- **A**
folution to his letter of yefterday, which anfwer is entirely comprehended in what I wrote you. You may
let him know that I fhall act confiftent with other circumftances that are now depending; but that I mean
to act entirely from my own feeling, but I thank him **B**
for his advice, and that my mind and actions are fixed,
after the moft deliberate reflection. If you are inclined that every thing fhould be carried through the
medium of your uncle, and not yourfelf only, let me
know it, and I will appoint fome friend of mine to act
for me, and anfwer to him. Decency and delicacy re- **C**
quire that you fhould infift on this with me, and not
have it faid that matters were done without my knowing whether they are as you wifh, and to your defire.
(A fhort paragraph torn off.)

Pleafe return the inclofed letters of your uncle's and **D**
my father's.

I have wrote to your mother by this poft, but not a
fyllable on this fubject or you, as I leave you to inform her all.

I muft requeft you will by courfe of poft fay you
have received this, elfe it will oblige me to go in **E**
fearch of this letter, even to London. It is not a fubject for every body's perufal. *Pleafe to let me know
what name you wifh to keep, that I may addrefs you accordingly.*

(Signed) C. C.

No. XIII.

Captain Campbell to his Wife.

Hilfea, Dec. 10th, 1788.

MY DEAREST FRIEND,

A   I HAVE this day received your note of yefterday. Mine to you of yefterday's date will by this time have explained my fentiments and refolutions, to which I now refer you, and to have done with the fubject.

  Had you correfponded with me, and let me know what you wifhed, I was moft readily inclined to do
B every thing you could have wifhed; but had you been writing to a flave, the manner you have addreffed me could not have been more infulting. I have bore it till I can bear it no longer. When I defired your advice relative to my writing to my father, it was becaufe I thought it unneceffary to write him at all. I know not
C even what you alluded to, what you meant by it: yet, becaufe you defired it, I would have done it, had you not put it out of my power. You made me make eonceffions to your uncle—for your fake I did it; when, at that time and this, I look upon his conduct moft unjuftifiable. I allude even previous to my being
D at White-houfe; and although you was fubjecting my feelings to the moft contemptible infult, it was merely intended to gratify the feelings of others and yourfelf, and at the fame time refolved on feparating.

  Whatever my affection for you might induce me to do, I never will fubmit to be trampled on by any
E man—not even though you wifh me to be fo fervile.—I conclude by referring you entirely to my letter of yefterday; and, my friend, allow me to have
feeling

feeling to actuate my decifion as well as you. *I am* **A**
now satisfied to believe it is your feeling, and for once in
our lives fince our marriage, we have one feeling, one fen-
timent—and we—part with such.

God protect you.

C. C.

———— —

No. XIV.

Captain Campbell to his Wife.

Hilfea, Dec. 14th, 1788.

MY DEAREST FRIEND,

I EXPECTED to have heard from you relative to **B**
my letter to you of the 9th inftant. It was not my
intention to have troubled you no more, but as our
orders for embarkation are now arrived, I fhall once
more addrefs you for the laft time.

The Warley, the Ocean, and the Sulivan India- **C**
men, are the fhips we embark in. The Captain of
the firft takes leave of the Directors on the 16th inft.
and is to be here immediately, the other two the 20th
inftant. As my ftay in this country now is but a few
days, it is abfolutely neceffary that the *papers* I wrote
you about fhould be prepared and figned, and not left **D**
to the laft moment to drive me to greater diftraction.
You have forced me, it muft be done. My duty with
the regiment will require more attention than I ever
will be able to pay. I therefore muft infift that our
tranfactions may be finally ended.

Your conduct long, long has hurt me. I mean **E**
your indifference—your want of confidence—your decifion always againft me—all has provoked me to un-

I

war-

A warrantable words and expressions, but unmeant to of-
fend—but they never can again.

Lastly, your conduct since I left Saddle to this
hour, has made greater impression on me than God
knows what time can erase. I thought they were not
B your feelings, but I am now convinced. To ease you
as well as myself, I embrace your first intention of *se-
parating. I tear you from my heart* — and from my
thoughts—but I cannot help loving you. We never, never more meet after this my decisive resolu-
C tion. I again request that you will immediately have
the papers drawn out, and keep me no longer in this
state of mind, in this servility.

C. C.

———

No. XV.

Captain Campbell to his Wife.

Hilsea, Dec. 29th, 1788.

D ON receipt of your last, I came to the resolution
(which every part of your conduct towards me ought
to have made me do before) of never seeing you again.
I have only now to observe your threats of publishing
I am ready to meet at any time, and my silence since
E then has proceeded *only* from a desire of allowing myself peace, and no longer subjecting myself to the in-
sults you have offered me.

As my wife, you are entitled to a share of my fortune, but as I have none, the sole reason of my not
F finally signing the separation, is not to deprive you of
any future advantage should I be fortunate; but as
soon as I have any thing worth your acceptance, then
you may rely on my bringing matters to a decision.

I some

I some time since wrote your mother of my resolu- A
tion, and my reasons for so doing, (but nothing to
your prejudice) it was that neither she, nor you, nor
any person should have reason to suppose that any future transactions should influence me to change my
sentiments of you, or pursue another mode of living. B
I do now most solemnly declare, that you shall, in
every respect, be the object of my future intentions;
at the same time I now tell you, that you may take
any *steps* you think proper, to *declare that we never
meet again.* C

I beg you to consider *me* your friend, a friend
that will *never have it in his heart to do justice to you*;
and depend upon *my word of honour*, that I never will
molest or give you a moment's pain or uneasiness, either by word or deed. I have only to recommend, D
that if any thing should *happen*, and that you should
change your *situation of life*, let me tell you as a
friend, that you must put more confidence in your
husband, treat him with affection and more respect,
this will not only endear you to him, but make you E
both happy.

I do not expect to remain in Europe many days;
I request of you, the last favour I have ever to ask of
you—never to think more of me—to forget I have
faults—to forget I *was your husband*, and never to F
put pen to paper to me now or hereafter—this is my
last to you for ever. Wishing you long, long continuance of health and everlasting happiness,

I remain,

Ever your most affectionate husband,

(Signed)   CHARLES CAMPBELL.

No.

No. XVI.

Captain Campbell to Major Hook.

Hilfea, Aug. 27, 1788.

My dear Friend,

A   I WAS this day made happy by your letter of yefterday, and it gives me great pleafure to hear that you are fafely arrived in Europe once more, and all your little ones in good health. It is not for want of inclination that I cannot comply with your defire of

B   accompanying you to Scotland, as I would not hefi-tate to embrace the opportunity was it in any degree poffible; fituated as I am, you may reft affured the object of my going, which you allude to, would be very pleafing to me, and I have only to regret that it lies

C   out of my power. I have every inclination to come to a perfect underftanding with a father, and to part on good terms, when the chances moft probably are that we never meet more. If inclination did not prompt me, it would be my intereft to wifh it; but I

D   affure you, laying every interefted view afide, I fhould feel it as an happy hour.

    You will naturally wifh to know my reafons, and the obftacles which prevent my accompanying you: in the firft inftance, from the ftate of the regiment I

E   am the only Captain at quarters, and in a few days the command of the regiment falls upon me: as our Lieu-tenant-colonel never refides here, in order to accom-modate another gentleman, Captain in the regiment, who is married, and goes to Scotland to bring his

F   lady here, I have undertaken the paymafter's accounts for him during his abfence, and are doubtlefs apprifed of the neceffity of my conftant attendance on this ac-count. Independent of thefe reafons, I would not

think

think it safe to be absent any time from the regiment, **A**
as we expect to leave this in the first ships, and should
there be a sudden order for embarkation, which happened before, and which most probably will happen
again, to keep the real intent as long as possible from
a raw body of men, would be hurrying me very much, **B**
and be attended with very great inconvenience to Mrs.
Campbell in preparing for any sudden embarkation,
provided I can arrange my affairs so as to be able to
take her with me. I hope, however, I shall see you
before you leave London, and if you will let me **C**
know when you are decided on going, I will be in
London for a day or so; let me know your address,
and believe me,

MY DEAR FRIEND,

Your most affectionate

(Signed)   CHARLES CAMPBELL.

XVII.

Captain Campbell to Major Hook.

Hilsea, Aug. 30, 1788.

MY DEAR FRIEND,

I AM just favoured with your letter of yesterday. **D**
With regard to the importance of going to Scotland,
it does not strike me so forcibly as it does you. My
friend, you ought to know my father's disposition
well; indeed, the last time you was in Europe you had
good reason. I cannot judge whether you have had **E**
any letter from him on the subject; but I have so repeatedly been disappointed from intercession of friends,

C   that

A that I am perfectly of opinion, that the less the subject is mentioned to my father, the sooner a perfect understanding will take place; and, indeed, at present I know of no great misunderstanding between us. My father, from his manner of living, has contracted dif-

B ferent ideas, and there is no harm in father and son not being of the same sentiments after a certain period of life; particularly in the situation our families are in: independent of this, I could not think of going to Scotland to make him a visit, unless he was previously

C prepared to expect ime, and that he expressed the wish *to me* himself, which I have ever told I at all times would be happy to embrace. It is consistent for sons, at all periods of life, to have due respect for parents; but parents are only parents while they act as such, and

D the moment they alter and are desirous of shewing themselves as parents, filial respect requires that every thing should be forgot—and my heart inclines me to forget that conduct, that I would not have expected even from my bitterest enemy. Though my father

E had not the early advantages of education, but entered early into life—from his great intercourse with mankind, and an experience acquired by long services, and success far exceeding his *once greatest ambition*, he ought to have curbed a disposition that he was certain

F would tend to divide his whole family, and which fatal experience has taught me to feel, and the whole world to see. You see, my dear Sir, I open my mind to you as a friend, though I was too young when I last saw you to remember more than the great atten-

G tion you shewed to me while a boy at school.—I hope after this you will not ask me more to go to Scotland. Even independent of my first reasons, the state of the regiment renders it perfectly incompatible for me to get away, nor is there one single officer of the regi-

H ment absent on leave.

Mrs. Campbell some little time ago had a wish to see her friends in that part of the world; and, perhaps, if it

would

would not be inconvenient to you, she would like to go as far A
as Edinburgh ; but on this subject I must refer you to her-
self entirely : for my own part, I am not partial to that
country, having been but very little in it ; nor have I a de-
sire of seeing it, unless to see my sister, whom I really be-
lieve to be a good woman. B

In regard to my prospects in India, I assure you I
go with the idea of spending my time as happy as I
can. I know there is nothing to be got in my profes-
sion in this country, something may by chance fall to
my share in India as it has to others : but think your- C
self, do you not believe that what you have acquired
is dearly bought, when you consider the period of time
you have been absent from your native soil? I go determined to like the country, because I cannot better
myself—because I am too young to be idle : but I af- D
sure you, was I ten years farther advanced in life, a very
little would satisfy me to remain in England : but at
present a *good deal* would not induce me to give up
my *supposed prospects* in India, or retire from an active
life. I wish to know when you purpose leaving Lon- E
don; as in all probability, in the course of a month
or less, I shall be obliged to be in London to send
down my cloaths, &c. &c. and to settle some little
matters that I have to do, as most probably I shall be
no more in London after it, and then only for two F
days.—I hope you will be able to make out your intended excursion to Ramsgate, as I am sure you will
make Mrs. Fraser, Mrs. Campbell, and all the family
very happy.

I am perfectly satisfied it is through your goodness G
of heart that you have proposed my going to Scotland, and I assure you I feel it so—believe me,

MY DEAR FRIEND,

Your most affectionate,

(Signed)   CHARLES CAMPBELL.

XVIII.

*Captain Campbell to Major Hook.**

White Houfe, Wednefday Night,
Eight o'Clock.

MY DEAR FRIEND,

I AM this moment arrived here from Inverary; I
am fo fatigued, that I cannot come on, but have fent
to ftop your proceeding till I arrive with you. It is
a long two days you have been in Kintyre, and my
feelings have been well tried, more than I ever expected. I have wrote Mrs. Campbell to meet me in
a chaife, after fhe has breakfafted, early. I have defired her to be alone, as I want it moft particularly,
therefore hope you will fee it done. Write me by her.
Till to-morrow adieu.

C. C.

No. XIX.

Captain Campbell to Major Hook.

Inverary, Friday Night.

MY DEAR FRIEND,

I AM come this length, and fet off to-morrow
morning for Glafgow. Alas! what has my rafhnefs
brought on my mind—I cannot defcribe—may you
be more calm, and your feelings more at peace—I

* The above is the threatening letter alluded to in the one of
the fame date from Captain Campbell to his wife.

fincerely

sincerely hope, and my Harriet—Alas! why did I **A**
write what I never meant, or never, never could have
expressed—she forgives—yes—but that is not enough to
quiet my feelings, conscious of having wrote what she
never deserved—I am quite overcome—farewell.

Your most affectionate,

(Signed)   CHARLES CAMPBELL.

———

XX.

Captain Campbell to Major Hook.

Edinburgh, Nov. 10th, 1788.

My dear Friend,

WHEN you reflect calmly on the disappointment **B**
of my not having accompanied you to Kintyre, when
you know the reflections, the feelings I have experienced, you will not then think me so culpable as I
may now appear to you; the undertaking of your
carrying my Harriet to Kintyre, I thought and felt **C**
most arduous after the fatality I had experienced, after
the manner my now living sister was treated there—
her husband told by common servants of the house,
that a certain woman had desired him to send her away.
The decision known to the world her husband had **D**
made, of never entering the doors while the same influence prevailed—the wishes of my sister to accept
any invitation to that country, but prevented by those
very feelings that has guided and overpowered my actions in this affair. Yes, my friend, I dreaded my **E**
Harriet remaining there longer than the two promised
days in that House that had obliged a poor unfortunate sister, broken-hearted, to put an end to her own
existence

A existence from the ill-treatment she received there, and at an early period of life. You was twenty years absent from that country, you know not what had passed, or what motives had determined all my nearest connections to avoid that country. Your affection

B for my father—your friendly desire for bringing on a reconciliation between father and son, induced you to act from your own sincere feelings. How could I have expected, after the pressing letters of my Harriet's father, the soft persuasions of her mother availed

C nothing, that you could have brought matters to a better bearing; yet notwithstanding this, I own nothing should have induced me to use harsh expressions to my Harriet—nothing should have induced me to have said a word to hurt the friend whose only object was

D my good—my interest—I wrote you of my feelings; I could not bring myself to write what I have now done—but I sent you a letter inclosed to my Harriet, telling you* of my intentions of going with you to Scotland; but why my Harriet should have thought

E it necessary for delicacy or appearance to conceal my wish, I cannot say—all might have been well with my father had I gone at first. I judged for the best when I followed, and even while in Edinburgh, I was advised by all since my wife was there, to go even but

F for a day. I had a letter from Mrs. Fraser saying, it would make her happy if I saw him, even should Harriet wait on the road for my return; however, all I can blame myself for is using a single harsh word to my dearest Harriet, for never did she merit it; but the

G agitation of my feelings urged me beyond the bounds of propriety—but I am the greatest sufferer—my Harriet knows me well, and forgives; yet I feel for what I have done, since my father has received her so kindly, and yet is inclined to forget all that has happened between him and me, I will write a most affectionate letter, and am happy to think it may avail, which I had

* N. B. No such letter; he threatens her that he would say so.

despaired

despaired of, had not your friendly affiftance over-pre- **A**
vailed. I have only now to add, that you, my dear
friend, after this candid explanation of my feelings,
and the caufes from whence they fprung, will do me
the juftice to put a better conftruction on my actions
in this affair than you have; at the fame time let me **B**
affure you, that no perfon can be more fenfible and
grateful for your kind endeavours, both for me and
my Harriet, than I am; had I come to Scotland with
you every thing would have been explained to you on
our journey before we reached my father.

Your's affectionately,

CHARLES CAMPBELL.

No. XXI.

Captain Campbell to Major Hook.

Brook-ftreet, Monday.

IT is impoffible that I can defcribe the feelings that **C**
have racked my mind for fome time paft, and that
you, who have acted in the moft affectionate manner
to the object of my affections, fhould have reafon to
think me ungrateful. Compofe your mind, that has
been fo long difturbed on your dear niece's account, **D**
and truft that hereafter all will be well. On the moft
ferious reflection, my actions will be guided towards
her whom you fo much feel for; I truft to God, fuch
as will be fatisfactory to you, and inftrumental to the
future happinefs of her I moft love. I would yet wifh **E**
to fee you, if you will permit me, before I leave London, which will be very foon.

Your affectionate
(Signed) CHARLES CAMPBELL.

No.

No. XXII.

Major Hook to Col: C. C. dated London, 1st September, 1788.

(After a paragraph on business.)

A   "I WOULD now proceed to indulge in a visit
"which I have long wished to have it in my power to
"pay, and as I cannot but feel myself sincerely inte-
"rested in every thing that concerns the happiness of
"an uncle, and the latter part of a life that has con-
B "ferred so many advantages on his relations, it shall
"be my unceasing study to mediate conciliation; and
"as there is so near an approach of a long separation
"between your son Charles, on the eve of embark-
"ing for India, and his good father, I could not help
C "asking him to accompany me, he tenderly expressed
"that such a meeting would be an happy hour, and
"with modest reserve left me to conclude that the un-
"certainty of his reception would prevent him.

    "Give me leave to beg of you on receipt of this,
D "to write him two lines, expressing a wish to see him
"before he sets out. I shall stay till I hear from you,
"or till he writes me that he has heard from you; he
"knows nothing of this letter, and I would wish
"to accommodate him in the trip. Poor fellow!
E "with a growing family his prospect is but dark. Let
"him have every encouragement that affectionate
"treatment can afford; I am certain such a meeting
"will be highly grateful to you hereafter, at those se-
"rious moments of reflection, which, sooner or later,
"we must all experience. Remember me, &c. &c.

                                        "A, H."

No. XXIII.

Colonel Charles Campbell to Major Hook.

Barr, 7th Sept. 1788.

MY DEAR ARCHY,

(Being all matters of bufinefs no ways connected, till)

. . . . . . AS to Charles, I would with pleafure A comply with your requeft of defiring him to accompany you here; was it not for very fubftantial reafons, which I doubt not will appear fatisfactory to you at meeting; therefore he had much better remain with his corps. Take your own method of mentioning this.

(Concludes upon bufinefs.)

Your uncle,
CHARLES CAMPBELL.

———

XXIV.

Colonel Charles Campbell to Major Hook.

YOUR card, my dear Archy, has furprifed and B aftonifhed me fo much, that I am quite unhinged and made almoft diftracted; not, I affure you, on account of Charles's conduct, becaufe it is all of a piece with his behaviour for ten years back; it is poor Harriet, whom I pity from the bottom of my heart, and who I declare I love as much as ever a man loved his

own

A own daughter, and whofe happinefs I have as much at heart as you could wifh; but, alas! at prefent, it is entirely out of my power to give her the confolation fhe fo much merits. I would comply moft chearfully with your defire in any thing but going to Saddle,

B which I would not take the world to do, becaufe I know my own temper fo much, that a meeting with Charles would be fuch as to expofe us both for ever to the talk of the world—In fhort, I am already almoft in a fever, and can fcarcely hold the pen in my hand.

C This attempt of his to force a reconciliation with me, exceeds all attempts ever made by mortal man; and not a perfon but himfelf would have thought of it: he muft now go back as faft as he came, for if he was to come here, or remain in the country twelve months,

E pofitively I would neither fpeak to him, or receive him into the houfe. You know I told you what a felfifh, opiniated, wavering, reftlefs difpofition, he had: in fhort, my dear Archy, nothing poffibly can ever re-form him, but a firm, fteady refolution not to give

F way to him in any refpect, for while a hope is left of yielding to him, there will be no end to his unreafona-blenefs. You have really a difagreeable tafk, and I pity you moft fincerely. I repeat, that Charles will never obtain either favour or countenance from me

G by following fuch conduct as hitherto; and he ought to know, from the intimation frequently made to him-felf, that I have done more for him than he deferves. To conclude, by Heavens, I will not fee him, nor ever correfpond with him, unlefs he returns inftantly.

H Love to Harriet.

I am, DEAR ARCHY,
Your moft affectionate,
Thurfday. CHARLES CAMPBELL.

P. S. In fhort, his treatment to me has been fuch as to make me hate to hear his name mentioned; and he miftakes himfelf and me very much, if he fuppofes he

can

can fhake my fixed refolution refpecting him :—no, **A**
by G—d, he fhall not ! and it requires but one ftep
more to make me declare to the world that I give him
up as a fon ; and if he dares to come near me at prefent, that declaration fhall be made.

———

XXV.

Colonel Campbell to Major Hook.

Friday night.

I HAVE, my dear Archy, received your's ; I can **B**
eafily conceive the diftrefs of mind you and poor Harriet muft have fuffered on account of Charles's conduct ; and forry am I to fay, that I have long obferved
fo much ficklenefs and overbearance in his difpofition, that no action man can be guilty of but I appre- **C**
hend from him ; and had not that been my opinion,
an opinion grounded upon years experience, I fhould
moft certainly have, long ere this, acted towards him
otherwife than I have done. I know many blamed me for
what they were pleafed to call cruel treatment ; but I **D**
cared not for that, as I was perfectly convinced, in my
own mind, that if I had acted otherwife, or yielded more
to the whims and unreafonablenefs of my fons, I was
undone ; and I have not a doubt, from what you have
feen and know of them, but you will now be perfuaded
I had too much caufe to act as I have done. Good Mrs.
Frafer's indulgence to him has done him no fervice ;
he took advantage of it, and treated her more like
mafter of the houfe than one under numberlefs obliga- **E**
tions :—in fhort, he has not fenfe to perceive betwixt
common civility and great kindnefs : his heart is con-

tinually

A tinually bent on something new, and he has the vanity to think he is intitled to direct every thing; that
his constant teasing and plagueing people will bring
every body to his way of thinking; and the very thing
which he would this night be perfectly contented to be in
B possession of, the next day he dislikes, and pants for
something new; and to you only do I tell it, that he
does not care much what he says or does to obtain his
wishes:—to be plain, he is a truly bad-hearted, deceitful lad, and I would not give two-pence for any pro-
C mise he makes, as I can assure you there is no reliance
to be put upon any thing he says; that, with one of
the worst tempers man ever possessed, gives a most melancholy chance of his ever reforming. I shall, however, write him what you desire; but rest assured, it
D will avail little, as I should not in the least be sur-
prised that, though he promised to allow Harriet to
remain in Europe, he repented the moment the ship
was to sail, and returned for her. For my own part,
I know no way of treating him, but not to give way to
E him in any thing; for when he takes it in his head,
that by obstinacy, passion, and fractiousness, he will
succeed, he will persevere; but if any body would shew
a disinclination to yield to his unreasonableness, he would
soon see his own folly; and the same disposition will
F make him behave to Harriet with cruelty, if she does
not summon courage to speak to him, and threaten to
demand a separation for bad usage. Consider of this,
and act accordingly. I really think you had better communicate to me on paper what you have to say, rather
G than come here, as your coming would occasion many
conjectures, some perhaps favourable, and some as
much to the contrary; and when you get to London,
let me know how he conducts himself. Be sure to let
Harriet keep the last threatening letter she got from
H Charles; for if matters come to an extremity, she can
shew reason for complaint against him. Mrs. Fraser
will now see, when too late, how much she was de-

2   ceived

ceived in him, and how little regard she paid to the **A**
opinion I gave her of him :—nay, I really believe she
was bewitched by him, for every thing he said to her
was gospel, and every fault I told her he had, she believed proceeded from my ignorance, or want of
knowledge of mankind. Had she treated him as a **B**
person dependent upon her good offices and friendship,
it would have humbled him, and made him less ty-
rannical ; but he found out her sweet, friendly temper,
and he has made a most ungenerous use of it. In
short, from my soul do I believe he does not care if **C**
she, me, and all that belonged to us, were in misery, so
he gets what he wanted by it. I also believe, from my
soul, that he is as bad a tempered man as exists, void
of affection and gratitude. I have said so much, that I
am assured you are tired and distressed at my opinion ; **D**
but to you I divulge the secrets of my heart. Comfort
I never had by sons, nor ever expect ; and I do not
know but even you might, before you were so well acquainted, with Charles and my other sons' dispositions,
think I was to blame ; but believe me, dear Archy, had **E**
I acted otherwise to such unfeeling beings, I might this
day be a beggar, as I am convinced it would give joy
to have all I am possessed of divided amongst them, if
I should starve. Farewell, love and blessings attend
you and Harriet.

Your most affectionate uncle,
CHARLES CAMPBELL.

———

No. XXVI.

Colonel Charles Campbell to Major Hook.

MY DEAR ARCHY,

THE accompanying is wrote that you may read it
to Charles, and it is positively my sentiments in every
respect,

A refpect, as I would not take the world and fpeak to
him. In fhort, his treatment to me has been fuch,
that I can fcarcely bear to hear his name mentioned;
notwithftanding which, to give Harriet all the comfort
in my power, if on his return to London he writes me
B fuch a letter as his conduct entitles me to expect, I
fhall write him back what we agreed upon. This is
all I can promife, and I truft when you fincerely confider what I faid to you concerning Charles, you
will not only pity me, but approve of my fixed deter-
C mination. Love and bleffings attend Harriet.
I ever am,
Your uncle,
CHARLES CAMPBELL.

P. S. I befeech my dear Harriet and you to put the
true conftruction on my refufing to comply with your
requeft. I repeat again and again, if I was to get the
whole univerfe I would not fee him. I fhall certainly
D write fhortly to Mrs. Frafer and Harriet. Charles's
conduct will never leffen my regard for them; on the
contrary, if you do not fhew firmnefs towards him, he
will have the vanity to think, that by continuing to
plague, he will at laft be fuccefsful; for that, I affure
E you, is his difpofition, and by it he has already loft
many good friends: nothing can reclaim him but
every body's convincing him he has nothing to depend
upon but his own good conduct. Mrs. Frafer ought
not to give too much way to his humours, for he will
F overbear and command with haughtinefs where he can.
Farewell, my dear Archy, Heaven preferve you from
fuch grief and heart-break from fons, as I am conftantly meeting with. The fooner and more privately
you get out of this country the better. Hard—hard
fate, to have fo unexpected and difagreeable a companion with you.
C. C.

No.

No. XXVII.

Colonel Campbell to Major Hook.

MY DEAR ARCHY,

I DELAYED thus long in expectation of hearing A of your arrival in London, which I hope happened before this time, without any accident to either you or poor Harriet. Inclosed is a letter for Charles, which, after perusing, you may deliver either open or sealed, as appears best to you; in it I have expressed B the sentiments of my heart, and what I am unalterably determined upon; and I think it better for both him and me to know what he has to depend upon, rather than be constantly plaguing my soul: and I am perfectly convinced, the stricter he is obliged to keep to C his duty, and the less hopes he has of pecuniary aid, the more he will attempt doing for himself, at least, if he has either prudence or ambition; for I know his restless begging disposition so well, that until he is made thoroughly sensible of the folly of depending D upon others for assistance, he never will exert himself like a man, so that he may be independent. I have hitherto said so much to him, and it has always been so much disregarded, that to tell you the plain truth, my hopes are by no means sanguine of his ever being what E I wish him to be. Good Mrs. Fraser must really summon courage and speak freely her sentiments to him; the goodness of her heart, and tender regard for her children, he has most certainly long since taken the advantage of, and treated her rather as one F dependent upon him than otherwise. And I repeat, he and all his brothers are of so arbitrary, overbearing tempers, that they will domineer over every person

who

A who will fubmit to it, and of all of them, he has not the leaft of that difpofition, as I doubt not, you have; long e'er now obferved. In fhort, my fole dependence on his acting at all properly, is from the impreffion your advice makes upon him, therefore, will fay no more on that fubject.

Your uncle,

CHARLES CAMPBELL.

Bar, 29th Nov. 1788.

This letter concludes with a paragraph upon money matters, not appertaining to the above.

AFFIDAVITS.

AFFIDAVITS.

JAMES CROSBY, of Thames Ditton, in the **A** county of Surrey, maketh oath and faith, that he knows Major Archibald Hook, and Captain Charles Collins Campbell, and Harriet his wife, and hath so known them for some years past: And this deponent faith, that he came from India with the said Major **B** Hook, and arrived in England on or about July, 1788, and lived with him till the April following: And this deponent further faith, that he accompanied the said Major Hook and Mrs. Campbell to Scotland, as far as Campbell-town, in Argyleshire, and returned **C** with them to Brook-street, and married in the said Major Hook's service about April, 1789, whereupon this deponent quitted his service, and set up a shop; but that not answering, he, this deponent, returned to the said Major Hook again in October, 1791, and lived **D** with him 12 months : And this deponent faith, that on the return of Major Hook and Mrs. Campbell from Scotland, the said Major Hook lived at a hotel till a house was taken at Walton, about which time he, this deponent, thinks that the said Major Hook **E** slept a few nights at Brook-street, but never before lived there, having lived at Kensington : This deponent further faith, that in the month of December,

E

1788,

A 1788, he accompanied the said Major Hook and Mrs. Campbell to Walton, about the middle of the month; that he, this deponent, always flept at the inn, and that after that they had been there a few days, Elizabeth Heron came down, and that he, this depo-

B nent, left Major Hook about the beginning of May, 1789; that Captain Campbell went to Hilfea from Brook-ftreet about the beginning of December, 1788, and never was at Walton while Mrs. Frafer lived there; that he, this deponent, in the month of July,

C 1791, accompanied Major Hook and Mrs. Campbell and family to Leoftoff, and returned to Twickenham, and remained with them till the month of October, 1791, when he, this deponent, quitted the said Major Hook's fervice: This deponent further faith,

D that he never faw any indecent or improper behaviour between the said Major Hook and Mrs. Campbell, nor did he ever fufpect any: And this deponent faith, that in travelling, and at all times, they, the said Major Hook and Mrs. Campbell, had always feparate apart-

E ments: This deponent further faith, that on or about the 14th day of November, 1792, one Samuel Jackfon, who had formerly been fervant to Mrs. Frafer, and now keeps the Betty Chop-houfe in the Strand, went to this deponent's houfe at Thames

F Ditton, and told him that Captain Campbell was with him, the said Jackfon, and at the inn: And this deponent faith, that he, Jackfon, accofted him as follows: " Crofby, I am come to you about a bufi-
" nefs in which, if you will fpeak the truth, it will be

G " pounds and pounds in your way. Have you not
" feen Major Hook frequently going into Mrs. Camp-
" bell's bed-room?"—To which this deponent made anfwer (expreffing his furprife at fuch queftion) yes, that he, this deponent, often faw Major Hook in Mrs.

H Campbell's room when other people were there alfo: And this deponent faith, that he, Jackfon, went to the inn where Captain Campbell then was, feemingly
much

much difappointed: This deponent further faith, that **A** the faid Jackfon came again to his houfe, on or about the 23d day of December, 1792, and after infinuating a great deal of what other people were to fay regarding the conduct of Major Hook and Mrs. Campbell, he, the faid Jackfon, again endeavoured to prevail on **B** him, this deponent, to fpeak: And this deponent further faith, that he was afterwards ordered in by Mr. Hawkins to the faid Jackfon's houfe, and that he, the faid Jackfon, faid to him, in the hearing of feveral of the witneffes, " Crofby, come, you feem low; I **C** " know you will fay the fame as other people when " you will appear at the trial; Major Hook knows he " will lofe the day; it is not the firft time I have " given ten guineas for an oath, for the beft people in " the land." This deponent further faith, that Major **D** Hook never lived at Brook-ftreet, but that he might have flept there two or three nights previous to his fetting off for Scotland.

JAMES CROSBY.

Sworn at Twickenham, this 11th day of March, 1793, before Hugh Cleghorn, Efq. One of His Majefty's Juftices of the Peace for the County of Middlefex.

HUGH CLEGHORN.

HENRY WHITEURST, of Duke-ftreet, Man- **E** chefter-fquare, in the county of Middlefex, gentleman, maketh oath and faith, that he knows Major Archibald Hook, and Captain Charles Collins Campbell, and Harriet his wife: And that this deponent faith, that on or about the month of October, 1789,

the

A the said Major Hook agreed with him, this deponent, for ready-furnished lodgings in his, this deponent's house, in Duke-street aforesaid, for him, the said Major Archibald Hook, and his niece, Mrs. Harriet Campbell: And this deponent further saith, that the

B said Major Archibald Hook, and Mrs. Harriet Campbell, accordingly entered upon, and lived in, the said lodgings, until the month of April following, during all which time, he, this deponent, never saw, or had any suspicion of, any improper intercourse or connec-

C tion by, or between the said Major Archibald Hook and Mrs. Harriet Campbell: And this deponent further saith, that he perfectly remembers, that one evening during the time, the said Major Archibald

D Hook, and Mrs. Harriet Campbell so lodged in his house, as aforesaid, the said Harriet Campbell was from home, from whence she went in a job-coach. One Robert Green, who was then servant to the said Major Archibald Hook, was sent out for the said

E Mrs. Campbell, but returned without finding her; upon which the said Major Hook requested this deponent to go to the coachman, and learn of him where he had left Mrs. Campbell; and this deponent saith he did so accordingly, but found that the coachman was gone to bed; that about eleven o'clock the said Mrs.

F Campbell came home, and shortly after ran into the street, and that Robert Green went after her, and brought her, the said Mrs. Campbell, back, and that she shut herself up in the parlour, and shortly after went up to her bed-room: And this deponent further

G saith, that he did not, on that evening, or at any other period of time whatever, hear the said Mrs. Campbell cry out murder, or the said Major Hook say to Mrs. Campbell, " You are a whore, a damned " whore, and the worst of whores;" nor any other expression or words to the like purport or effect: And this deponent saith, that on the said evening above-mentioned and alluded to, there were in

2   his

his, this deponent's houfe, with him, this deponent, **A**
Alice Jones, his niece, and Elizabeth White, his fervant: And this deponent further faith, that his houfe
is but fmall, and believes, that no expreffions, delivered
in a violent tone of voice, in any part of the houfe,
could poffibly be ufed, without his, this deponent, or **B**
Alice Jones, or Elizabeth White's, hearing them:
And this deponent faith, that in his, this deponent's,
houfe, regular hours were kept, and that fome one of
the family was always at home: And further faith, **C**
that had any indecent expreffions, or improper behaviour, been either heard or feen, between the faid Major Hook and Mrs. Campbell, he, this deponent, would
not have fuffered them to remain in his houfe: And
this deponent further faith, that he remembers a print
fhop-man coming repeatedly to the faid Major Hook, **D**
whilft he was at his, this deponent's houfe, demanding
payment from the faid Major Hook for fome prints,
which had been bought of him by one Jofeph Rippington, fervant to the faid Major, which he, the faid
Major Hook, on fuch demands, always refufed paying **E**
for: And this deponent remembers the faid Jofeph
Rippington's faying, that it was hard that he, (the faid
Jofeph Rippington) fhould be obliged to pay for them
himfelf: And this deponent further faith, that a gentleman, whom he fuppofed to be Mr. Hawkins, at- **F**
torney for the faid Captain Campbell, called upon him,
this deponent, in Duke-ftreet, and addreffed himfelf to
this deponent, by ftating to him, that when Major
Hook had run away with Mrs. Campbell from her
mother's houfe, he brought her to Duke-ftreet, to his, **G**
this deponent's, houfe, and there lived with her; upon
hearing which, he, this deponent, told the faid Mr.
Hawkins, that in his, this deponent's, opinion, that
could not be true, as Mrs. Campbell's mother, brother, and fifters, frequently vifited them, and that the **H**
fifters

(38)

A sisters used frequently to stay several days and nights with Mrs. Campbell.

H. WHITEHURST.

Sworn at London, in the County of Middlesex, this 13th day of March, 1793, before Hugh Cleghorn, Esq. One of His Majesty's Justices of the Peace for the County of Middlesex.

HUGH CLEGHORN.

THE voluntary declaration and deposition of ELIZABETH WHITE, who upon her oath saith, that she lived in Mr. Whitehurst's house, in Duke-street, when Major Hook and Mrs. Campbell lived there, from the month of October, 1789, to the end of April the following year, and saith, that she never saw any thing improper between Major Hook and Mrs. Campbell: She further saith, that she never called Robert Green into Mrs. Campbell's bed-room, nor observed to him the marks of two people having lain on Mrs. Campbell's bed; and further declares, that she never saw such marks, nor had any suspicion of them, and that she always made Mrs. Campbell's bed: And further saith, that Mrs. Whitehurst, in consequence of some observations of Robert Green's, desired her and Alice Harpur to observe, which they did accordingly, and informed her, that they had never seen any thing improper: And further saith, that she remembers the night on which Mrs. Campbell went into the street, when Robert Green went after her, and brought her back,

back, and when she shut herself up in Mr. Whitehurst's A parlour: She further saith, that she was with Mrs. Campbell on the stair, and attended her up to bed, and did not then, or at any other time, hear Major Hook make use of the following expressions, "You are a "whore, a damned whore, and the worst of whores:" B And this deponent further saith, that no such expressions could have been used by Major Hook to Mrs. Campbell at that time without her hearing them, because she was never a moment absent from Mrs. Campbell, from the time she fell on the stair until she, C this deponent, put Mrs. Campbell to bed: And this deponent further saith, that she did not, on that night, or on any other, during Major Hook's residence in Duke-street, hear the cry of murder: And further saith, that she heard Robert Green say, "That he would make D "Major Hook suffer for it, if he would turn him "away; and that he would find ways and means to "make the old rascal's money fly." This deponent further saith, that Mr. Whitehurst, Alice Harpur, (his niece) and this deponent, were in the house on that E night; but that the threat about making his money fly was said to her alone in the scullery.

ELIZABETH WHITE.

Sworn at Brentford, this
9th day of March,
1793, before Hugh
Cleghorn, Esq. One of
His Majesty's Justices
of the Peace for the
County of Middlesex.

HUGH CLEGHORN.

MAR-

A   ALICE JONES, of Duke-ftreet, Manchefter-
fquare, in the county of Middlefex, maketh oath, and
faith, that fhe knows Major Archibald Hook, and
Captain Charles Collins Campbell, and Harriet his
wife: And this deponent faith, that fhe lived with Mr.
B Henry Whitehuruft, of Duke-ftreet, at the fame time
when the faid Major Hook and Mrs. Campbell came
and took lodgings in the faid Mr. Whitehurft's houfe,
and that fhe, this deponent, was in the fame houfe all
the time that the faid Major Hook and Mrs. Camp-
C bell lived in the faid lodgings, during all which time
fhe, this deponent, never faw any indecent or improper intercourfe between the faid Major Hook and Mrs.
Campbell: And this deponent further faith, that fhe
remembers one evening during the time the faid Ma-
D jor Hook and Mrs. Campbell had the faid lodgings as
aforefaid, that Mrs. Campbell ran out of the houfe
into the ftreet, about eleven o'clock at night, and that
Robert Green went after her, and brought her the faid
Mrs. Campbell back, when fhe the faid Mrs. Camp- .
E bell went into the parlour: And this deponent further
faith, that fhe did not hear the faid Mrs. Campbell, or
any other perfon, cry out murder; nor did fhe this deponent hear the faid Major Hook, either that evening, or at any other time whatever, fay to the faid
F Mrs. Campbell, " You are a whore, a damn'd whore,
" and the worft of whores :" And this deponent alfo
faith, that the abovementioned houfe is fmall, and
that Mrs. Whitehurft, Betty White, and herfelf, this
deponent, who lived there during the faid Major Hook
G and Mrs. Campbell's refidence in the faid houfe, were
very quiet and regular in their hours: And fhe this
deponent thinks, that if any fuch expreffions had been
ufed

uſed, ſhe muſt have heard them, which ſhe this depo- **A** nent declares ſhe did not.

ALICE JONES.

Sworn at London, in the
County of Middleſex, this
3d Day of April, 1793,
before Hugh Cleghorn,
Eſq. One of his Ma-
jeſty's Juſtices of the
Peace for the County of
Middleſex.

HUGH CLEGHORN.

MARGARET BUCHAN, Cook to Major Hook, **B** maketh oath and ſaith, that ſhe knows the ſaid Major Archibald Hook, and Captain Charles Collins Campbell, and Harriet his wife: And this deponent ſaith, that ſhe entered into the ſaid Major Hook's ſervice in the year 1791, in the month of October, and conti- **C** nued in it till the May following; and that ſhe never ſaw, or heard, or even ſuſpected any thing improper between the ſaid Major Hook and Mrs. Campbell.

M. B.

Sworn this 11th day of
March, 1793, at Twick-
enham, before Hugh Cleg-
horn, Eſq. One of His
Majeſty's Juſtices of the
Peace for the County of
Middleſex.

HUGH CLEGHORN.

F   FLORA

A   FLORA STEWART, native of India, and fer-
vant-maid to Major Hook, maketh oath, and faith,
that fhe knows the faid Major Archibald Hook, and
Captain Charles Collins Campbell, and Harriet his
wife; that fhe lived many years with the faid Major
B Hook, and came from India with him: And this deponent faith, that fhe was at Walton during the time
• that the faid Major Hook and Mrs. Campbell were
there, and that the faid Mrs. Campbell was in a bad
ftate of health: And this deponent faith, that fhe ne-
C ver faw or fufpected any improper conduct between
the faid Major Hook and Mrs. Campbell: And this
deponent further faith, that at Eaft Bourn bathing-
place, where fhe accompanied the faid Major Hook
and Mrs. Campbell, and the family, fhe, this depo-
D nent, and Maria Stewart, another native of India,
flept on the fame floor with Mrs. Campbell, and that
fhe, this deponent, neither there or any where elfe, at
any time, ever faw or heard any improper behaviour
or expreffions between the faid Major Hook and Mrs.
E Campbell: And this deponent further faith, that Jane
Grimes, who was then cook, never told her, while at
Eaft Bourn, that fhe, the faid Grimes, had feen or
heard any thing improper. This deponent faith, that
fhe doth not remember when fhe went to Walton, nor
F can fhe fpeak as to time; and that fhe could not fpeak
or underftand much Englifh when fhe came home,
and but very little of it even now: And this deponent
further faith, that at Eaft Bourn the faid Mrs. Campbell and Mifs Hay, with Major's Hook's two daugh-
G ter's, flept in one room, and that Major Hook and his
fon flept together in the next; and that Maria Stewart
flept with this deponent in the room oppofite to that
in which the faid Major Hook and his fon flept: She
further

further faith, that Jane Grimes and the man-fervant, A
Arthur Bane, flep on the garret.

her
FLORA   +   STEWART,
mark.

Sworn at Twickenham,
this 11th day of March,
1793, before Hugh Cleg-
horn, Efq. One of His
Majefty's Juftices of the
the Peace for the County
of Middlefex.

HUGH CLEGHORN,

MARIA STEWART, native of India, and fer- B
vant-maid to Major-Hook, maketh oath and faith, that
fhe knows the faid Major Archibald Hook, and Captain Charles Collins Campbell, and Harriet his wife;
that fhe lived many years with the faid Major Hook,
and came from India with him: And this deponent
faith, that fhe was at Walton during the time that the C
faid Major Hook and Mrs. Campbell were there; and
that the faid Mrs. Campbell was in a bad ftate of
health: And this deponent faith, that fhe never faw or
fufpected any improper behaviour between the faid
Major Hook and Mrs. Campbell: And this deponent D
further faith, that at Eaft Bourn bathing-place, where
fhe accompanied the faid Major Hook, Mrs. Campbell, and family, fhe, this deponent, and Flora Stewart,
another native of India, flept on the fame floor with
Mrs. Campbell; and that fhe, this deponent, neither
there nor any where elfe, at any time, ever faw or heard E
any improper conduct, or expreffions, between the faid

F 2   Major

A Major Hook and Mrs. Campbell: And this deponent further faith, that Jane Grimes, who was then cook, never told her, while at Eaſt Bourn, that ſhe, the ſaid Grimes, had ſeen or heard any thing improper: And this deponent ſaith, that ſhe does not remember when
B ſhe went to Walton, nor can ſhe ſpeak as to time; and that ſhe could not ſpeak nor underſtand much English when ſhe came home, and but very little of it even now: And this deponent further ſaith, that at Eaſt Bourn the ſaid Mrs. Campbell and Miſs Hay, with
C Major Hook's two daughters, ſlept in one room, and that Major Hook and his ſon ſlept together in the next, and that Flora Stewart ſlept with this deponent in the room oppoſite to that in which Major Hook and his ſon ſlept: And this deponent further ſaith,
D that Jane Grimes and Arthur Bane, the man-ſervant, ſlept in the garret.

her

MARIA + STEWART,

mark.

Sworn at Twickenham, this 11th day of March, 1793, before Hugh Cleghorn, Eſq. One of His Majeſty's Juſtices of the Peace for the County of Middleſex.

HUGH CLEGHORN.

E MARY CROSBY, of Thames Ditton, in the county of Surry, maketh oath and ſaith, that ſhe knows Major Archibald Hook, and Captain Charles Collins Campbell, and Harriet his wife: And this deponent

ponent faith, that fhe lived with Mrs. Frafer at Wal- A
ton: and that fhe, this deponent, ufed to affift in
making the beds; that fhe never faw any thing indecent or improper between the faid Major Hook and
Mrs. Campbell: And this deponent further faith, that
fhe afterwards lived with Major Hook and Mrs. B
Campbell at Twickenham, and accompanied them to
Loeftoff fea-bathing, and returned with them, the faid
Major Hook and Mrs. Campbell, to Twickenham,
and left Major Hook's fervice in the month of October, 1791; during which time, this deponent faith, C
that fhe never faw, or even fufpected, any indecent or
improper behaviour between the faid Major Hook
and Mrs. Campbell: And this deponent further faith;
that on or about the 14th day of November, 1792,
one Samuel Jackfon, who had been formerly fervant
to Mrs. Frafer, and now keeps the Betty chop-houfe in D
the Strand, came to her houfe at Thames Ditton, and,
in the deponent's hearing, faid to her hufband, James
Crofby, " Crofby, I am come about a piece of bufi-
" nefs, in which, if you fpeak truth, it will be pounds
" and pounds in your way: Have you not feen Major
" Hook in Mrs. Campbell's bed-room?" with other E
words and expreffions to the fame effect: And this
deponent further faith, that on or about the 23d of
December, 1792, he, the faid Samuel Jackfon, came
again to her houfe, with Mr. Hawkins's clerk, and
after fhewing papers, which they faid contained the F
depofitions of other witneffes relative to Major Hook,
they endeavoured, by queftions and other expreffions,
to induce them, the faid James Crofby, and this deponent, to fpeak on the fame fide: And this deponent
faith, that fhe and her hufband were both afterwards G
ordered in by Mr. Hawkins, to the faid Jackfon's
houfe: And that he, the faid Jackfon, faid to James
Crofby, this deponent's hufband, in the hearing of feveral of the witneffes, " Come, Crofby, drink, you
" will fay the fame as the reft, I know, when it comes
" to

A " to the point: it is not the firſt time I have given
" ten guineas for an oath, for the beſt man in the
" land:" and words to the ſame effect: And this deponent further ſaith, that ſhe had almoſt conſtant opportunity of obſerving the conduct of the ſaid Major
B Hook and Mrs. Campbell, and never ſaw or obſerved
the leaſt improper behaviour.

MARY CROSBY.

*Sworn at Twickenham,
this 11th day of March,
1793, before Hugh Cleg-
horn, Eſq. One of His
Majeſty's Juſtices of the
Peace for the County of
Middleſex.*

HUGH CLEGHORN,

———————

MISS MARY HAY, of Hammerſmith, in the
C county of Middleſex, maketh oath and ſaith, that ſhe
knows Major Archibald Hook, and Captain Charles
Collins Campbell, and Harriet his wife: And this
deponent ſaith, that on the 27th June, 1792, ſhe accompanied the ſaid Major Hook, and Mrs. Campbell,
D and family, to Eaſt Bourn bathing-place, where they,
the ſaid Major Hook, Mrs. Campbell, and this deponent, remained till about the 27th day of July following: And this deponent further ſaith, that while at
Eaſt Bourn, the ſaid Mrs. Campbell and Major Hook's
E daughters, and ſhe, this deponent, ſlept in one room,
and that the ſaid Major Hook and his ſon ſlept in an
adjoining room: And this deponent further ſaith, that

I   two

two women, natives of India, flept on the fame floor A
in a room oppofite to that in which the faid Major
Hook and his fon flept, and that the fervant-man and
a cook-maid (commonly called Jane) flept in the garret apartments: And this deponent faith, that fhe was
conftantly with the faid Mrs. Campbell and Major B
Hook's daughters, and that they, the faid Mrs.
Campbell, and Major Hook's daughters, and this deponent, ufed to bathe in the morning before breakfaft,
and from that time till dinner generally employed hearing the faid Major Hook's children reading and prac- C
tifing mufic and dreffing for dinner, and that in the
evening they commonly walked: And this deponent
further faith, that neither then at Eaft Bourn, nor at
any other time when fhe had been at Major Hook's
houfe, did fhe fee or hear, or had reafon to fuppofe, D
any thing inconfiftent with the higheft honour and the
moft refined practice of virtue.

MARY HAY.

*Sworn at Hammerfmith,
this 12th Day of March,
1793, before Hugh Cleg-
horn, Efq. one of His
Majefty's Juftices of the
Peace for the County of
Middlefex.*

HUGH CLEGHORN.

———————

MRS. MAGDALINE LOGOUX, of Harley- E
ftreet, in the county of Middlefex, maketh oath, and
faith, that fhe knows Major Archibald Hook, and
Cap-

A   Captain Charles Collins Campbell, and Harriet his
wife, and hath so known them for some years past;
and this deponent saith, that she went to live with Mrs.
Frafer, the mother of the said Mrs. Campbell, some
time in the month of February, 1788, as governess

B   to Mrs. Frafer's youngest daughters, at which time
Captain Campbell and Mrs. Campbell were living
with Mrs. Frafer, and this deponent continued in Mrs.
Frafer's family for three years, or thereabout: And
this deponent further saith, that very soon after she

C   went to live with Mrs. Frafer as aforesaid, she observed
that Captain Charles Campbell and Mrs. Campbell
were upon very bad terms; and that as her chamber
was near the room in which they, the said Captain
Campbell and Mrs. Campbell slept, she, this depo-

D   nent, often heard violent quarrels between them after
they had retired to their chamber, and that on one of
those occasions, Mrs. Frafer was obliged to go to
them, the said Captain Campbell and Mrs. Campbell, and take the said Mrs. Campbell into the said

E   Mrs. Frafer's room, and that the said Mrs. Campbell
was very ill for the greatest part of the night; that
Mrs. Campbell was in general so much affected with
those quarrels, that Mrs. Frafer was frequently obliged
to remain with her some time after them: And this

F   deponent saith, that not wishing to pry into family
concerns, is not particular as to the cause of such
quarrels, but that they were very frequent: And this
deponent further saith, that Captain Charles Collins
Campbell did not pay that attention to Mrs. Harriet

G   Campbell his wife, which this deponent thinks she, the
said Mrs. Campbell, deserved, and that he was very
much from home, and often staid out till two o'clock
in the morning: And this deponent also saith, that
Captain Charles Campbell left Brook-street about the

H   beginning of December 1788, and never visited Mrs.
Campbell, (who afterwards lived at Mrs. Frafer's
house

houfe at Walton) as this deponent verily believes : A
And this deponent further faith, that whilft he, Captain Campbell, was fo abfent from the faid Mrs. Campbell his wife, there were frequent quarrels between
Mrs. Frafer and Mrs. Campbell, and that they generally happened after they, the faid Mrs. Campbell and B
Mrs. Frafer, had received letters from Captain Charles
Collins Campbell, and that Mrs. Campbell was frequently indifpofed in confequence of fuch quarrels,
and that her health vifibly fuffered by them : And this
deponent faith, that the faid Mrs. Campbell endea- C
voured to conceal her fituation from the world, and
this deponent verily believes that no perfon, except
Mrs. Frafer (mother to Mrs. Campbell) knew what
fhe, Mrs. Campbell, really fuffered : And alfo faith,
that Captain Charles Collins Campbell feemed to her, D
this deponent, to be of a jealous temper ; and that
he, the faid Captain Charles Collins Campbell, could
not bear the fmalleft attention to be paid to her, Mrs.
Campbell : And this deponent further faith, that from
her fituation in the family fhe, this deponent, had E
more opportunities of obferving the conduct of Major
Hook and Mrs. Campbell, after they went to live at
Walton, than any of the fervants : And alfo faith,
that fhe, this deponent, was almoft conftantly with
the faid Mrs. Campbell, and went very often into her F
bedchamber, and fometimes in the middle of the
night : And this deponent further faith, fhe never obferved the leaft impropriety of conduct on the part of
the faid Major Archibald Hook towards Mrs. Campbell, but that he was very kind and attentive to the G
whole family, and feemed to this deponent to treat
the faid Mrs. Campbell and her fifters, more like a
good father than a more diftant relation : And this
deponent further faith, that Major Hook had been
frequently at Brook-ftreet, but did not live with Mrs. H
Frafer till fhe went to Walton, he, the faid Major

G   Hook,

A Hook, having had then a houfe of his own at Kenfington.

MAGDALINE LOGOUX.

Sworn at London, in the
County of Middlefex, this
12th Day of March,
1793, before Hugh Cleg-
horn, Efq. one of His
Majefty's Juftices of the
Peace for the County of
Middlefex.

HUGH CLEGHORN.

B   HARRIET CAMPBELL, of the county of
Surry, maketh oath and faith, that fhe remembers the
circumftance of her peevifh and petulant behaviour to
her uncle at Duke-ftreet, and that fhe went out one
day in a job coach, and remained out till about 11
C o'clock at night, that fhe is not quite pofitive as to the
hour, that fhe returned home in a hackney coach, having fent home the job coach before: That fhe remembers on her uncle's beginning to find fault with
her, and attempting to take hold of her hand, fhe, in
D a violent tone of voice, exclaimed—"Don't touch
"me, I'll do as I pleafe,"—or to that effect, and ran
down ftairs and went into the ftreet; that the fervant
(Green) came after her, and fhe immediately returned,
went firft into one of the parlours, and then went up
ftairs: That the fervant, Elizabeth White, attended
E her to bed, and that her uncle fpoke to her about her
foolifh behaviour; fhe offered fome kind of excufe for
having vexed him, upon which he made ufe of fome
warm expreffion, alluding to her fituation with refpect
to Captain Campbell's mother and relations. She
pofi-

positively denies having heard the expreſſion from Major Hook which the ſervant, Robert Green, has ſworn to: and ſhe ſolemnly declares, by this oath, that Major Hook never committed with her the crime of which he has been accuſed, but ever acted the part of a good and tender father to her in the ſtricteſt ſenſe.

HARRIET CAMPBELL.

Sworn at London, this 26th
Day of March, 1793,
before me, one of His
Majeſty's Juſtices of the
Peace for the County of
Middleſex.

HUGH CLEGHORN.

WILLIAM PAXTON, Eſq. of Queen's-ſquare, Bloomſbury, in the county of Middleſex, maketh oath and ſaith, that he knows Major Archibald Hook and Mrs. Harriet Campbell: And this deponent ſaith, that his acquaintance with the ſaid Major Archibald Hook is nearly of nineteen years ſtanding, during all which time he, this deponent, had frequent opportunities of obſerving the conduct and character of the ſaid Major Archibald Hook: And he, this deponent, further ſaith, that he ever found both eminently diſtinguiſhed by a moſt ſcrupulous attention to every principle of virtue, integrity, delicacy, and honour: And this deponent further ſaith, that the above is not only the reſult of his own obſervations, but what he, this deponent, ever underſtood to be the ſaid Major Hook's general character; and he alſo ſaith, that he, this deponent, never heard even the ſlighteſt inſinuation to the contrary from any perſon

G 2   what-

A whatever: And this deponent faith, that the faid Major Hook, with his three children, (on whofe welfare his very exiftence feemed to depend) arrived in England in the month of July, 1788, and that his mind, from family diftreffes, was in his, this deponent's opi-
B nion, grievoufly afflicted, and his conftitution, from the fame caufe, as well as a long refidence in India, impaired to fuch a degree, that the commiffion of a crime of a lefs heinous nature than that with which he the faid Major Archibald Hook is charged, is in his,
C this deponent's opinion, highly improbable: And this deponent, to evince the character of delicacy which he hath long fince fo juftly formed, and herein gives of the faid Major Hook, faith, that on this late occafion, when his all was at ftake, and it appeared that
D the teftimony of a young lady would have been of the utmoft importance, he, the faid Major Hook, declined to fubpœna her to court from motives of delicacy, notwithftanding the preffing remonftrances of friends and profeffional gentlemen to the contrary:
E And this deponent further faith, that he faw the faid Mrs. Campbell with Major Hook in Wales, and has frequently feen her fince in the faid Major Hook's houfe, and never obferved in the conduct of either the faid Mrs. Campbell or Major Hook, any thing
F but what was conformable in his, this deponent's, opinion, to the ftricteft rules of propriety as uncle and niece.

WILLIAM PAXTON.

Sworn in London this 15th Day of March, 1793, before Hugh Cleghorn, Efq. one of His Majefty's Juftices of the Peace for the County of Middlefex.

HUGH CLEGHORN.

No.

No. I.

From Colonel Ironside.

No. 29, Upper Brook-street, March 16, 1793.

SIR,

I RECEIVED your letter of the 15th inftant, and **A** very readily accede to the requeft it contains.

No gentleman with whom I had the honour to ferve, bore a fairer repute than Major Hook, for worth, and for refpeét and attention to thofe moral duties and obligations, which conftitute the valuable intercourfe **B** of focial life.

I have, &c.

(Signed)   GILBERT IRONSIDE.

———

No. II.

From Colonel Blair.

Stratford Place, No. 5, March 27, 1793.

SIR,

I HAVE received your letter of the 15th inftant, **C** in anfwer to which I have no difficulty in declaring, that whilft I ferved in India, I always underftood your conduét to have been that of an officer and a gentleman ; nor have I ever heard, during my refidence

A dence in that country, reflections of any kind against your moral character.

I am, &c.

WILLIAM BLAIR.

No. III.

From Colonel Duff.

London 23d March, 1793.

SIR,

B   IN reply to your letter of the 15th instant, I declare, that during the time I had the honour to serve with you in India, no man bore a higher character for honour, and all the principles of a gentleman, than you did ; and I am persuaded every person who served with you will readily confirm the same.

SIR, &c.

PATRICK DUFF.

No. IV.

From Captain Thomas Blair.

Welbeck-street, 16th March, 1793.

SIR,

C   IF my declaration can in the smallest degree tend to remove improper impressions against you, I now
give

give you my permiffion to declare, that during my **A**
refidence in Bengal for nearly twenty years, I neither
know or ever heard of any the moft diftant imputa-
tions againft your moral character.

SIR, &c.

THOMAS BLAIR.

No. V.

From Captain Howe.

London, March 22, 1793.

SIR,

I HAVE pleafure in faying, that during a refi- **B**
dence in India of between fixteen and eighteen years,
I never directly or indirectly heard a fyllable which
could in any wife impeach your moral character, and
if this teftimony can be ufeful to you in what you are
about to publifh, I fhall be happy to fee it made ufe **C**
of.

SIR, &c.

J. HOWE.

No. VI.

From Major Scott.

26th March, 1793.

SIR,

THOUGH our fituation in the army when we
ferved about twenty years ago, kept us afunder, yet

2 I cer-

A I certainly have had every opportunity of knowing the eſtimation in which you ſtood with all the officers, and no one in the army bore a fairer character as a moral man and a good officer; this teſtimony I bear with the utmoſt readineſs, and ever am,

SIR, &c.

JOHN SCOTT.

No. VII.

From Charles Cockerell, Eſq.

No. 7, *Saville Row,* 1793.

SIR,

B IT having been intimated to me by a particular friend, an acquaintance of yours, that under the circumſtance of the deciſion lately paſſed againſt you in one of the civil courts at law, ſome teſtimony to your conduct whilſt in India, from thoſe who had the
C pleaſure of your acquaintance in that country, would be acceptable to you; I cannot delay a moment not only to expreſs my concern at what has occaſioned, but to aſſure you that I know no perſon whoſe conduct had been conſidered as more attentive to, and
D tenacious of the ſtricteſt obſervance of every moral duty which can tend to enhance the value of the ſociety where we live, than that of yourſelf whilſt in India.

SIR, &c.

CHARLES COCKERELL.

TRIAL.

T R I A L.

In the King's Bench,

Feb. 26, 1793.

CAMPBELL against HOOK, Esq.

MR. *Holroyd.* May it please your Lordship, **A**
Gentlemen of the Jury, Charles Collins Campbell is
the plaintiff, and Archibald Hook the defendant. The
declaration complains, that the defendant made an
assault upon the wife of the plaintiff, and debauched,
lay with, and carnally knew her, and likewise that he **B**
has taken her away: whereby he has lost the comfort
and assistance of his wife, to his damage of 50,000l.
The defendant has pleaded, he is not guilty, upon
which the issue is joined.

Mr. *Erskine.* May it please your Lordship, Gen- **C**
tlemen of the Jury, I am of counsel for the plaintiff,
Mr. Campbell; and though I feel upon this occasion
for the unfortunate situation of my client, as my fide-
lity in this place requires I must state it : yet, as it
suggests itself to me, I will fairly admit to you, if I **D**
could discharge from my mind the painful sensations

H   he

A he muſt have had, if this cauſe had been poſtponed, or entirely put to an end, I ſhould have derived particular ſatisfaction, as far as perſonally concerns myſelf. I do not know a more painful ſenſation that belongs to an advocate, to ſtate a caſe that muſt bring reproach

B upon human nature itſelf; which, if proved, ſtrikes at all the confidence and comfort of human life.

Gentlemen, the defendant, who is charged with criminal converſation with the wife of the plaintiff, is an uncle of the lady—not an uncle by marriage, but her

C mother's brother. That I am perſuaded is ſufficient to engage all your attention, and excite your indignation in the cauſe.

I am informed the adultery and the inceſt is to be denied, and that denial is to be inſiſted on as a principal part of the defence; for what other can exiſt, I

D cannot tell. I have no difficulty in ſtating and conceding to my learned friend, it ought to be perfectly eſtabliſhed in proof: but I, in point of fact, ſhall prove the adultery, and not waſte your time or mine in ſta-

E ting preliminary obſervations upon the nature of the caſe; all I ſhall do, will be to ſtate the circumſtances, ſo that you may underſtand the evidence.

Gentlemen, the plaintiff, Mr. Campbell, is a Captain of the 74th regiment, a ſon of Colonel Camp-

F bell, of Campbell-town, Argyleſhire.

The lady was born about the year 1770, or 1771, and married in 1786; is the daughter of a Colonel Fraſer, in the Eaſt India Company's ſervice; was moſt religiouſly educated and brought up in morals, that

G unfortunately, however, have not been proof againſt the ſeduction of this relation.

It appears that Mr. Campbell being appointed to his regiment, that was raiſing in Scotland, it became neceſſary for him to attend on the recruiting ſer-

H vice. Afterwards, his regiment was ordered to the Eaſt Indies. His wife, with whom he was living in the greateſt affection, was to accompany him, and

Colonel

Colonel Fraser's lady being to accompany them to Hilsea barracks, at least it was expected the lady of Colonel Fraser would have been there. When Captain Campbell came to Hilsea barracks to settle his affairs, and his wife was to accompany him to the East Indies, there was no reluctance on her part, to going; she said it was painful to part with her mother, but she was desirous to go with her husband. Whilst the plaintiff was at Hilsea barracks, the defendant, a Major in the East India Company's service, returned to England with a considerable fortune : when he came back to this country, he found his own niece under the protection of her mother, the husband, the plaintiff, being absent.

Gentlemen, one is sorry to lay any charge of a criminal nature against any body ; I am sorry to be obliged, professionally, to lay such a charge against any individual, much more when it is a crime against human nature which we all wear and carry about us ; but the cause is such as obliges me to state it.

The moment the defendant came to England, he conceived the diabolical purpose of debauching her from her husband. *So early was the plan of seduction on the part of the uncle,* that the husband found, before the uncle had been three weeks in England, a difference in the stile of her letters. She began to raise obstacles against going to the East Indies. There was something dreadful and astonishing in the stile of those letters, and he could not guess what the meaning of it was, it did not occur to his mind—how should it ? How was it possible he could conceive there could be any criminal intercourse with her uncle ? yet he saw she was under his influence, and she was to take a journey to Scotland under pretence of visiting the father. Without making any farther animadversions upon it, that which took place was, that notwithstanding all he could do, his wife was adverse and contrary to his inclinations, and the advice of the uncle had led

her

A her mind to obey his will and inclinations inftead of her hufband's.

Soon after this the plaintiff embarked with his regiment to the Eaft Indies. The defendant had had the art to procure even the father of Captain Campbell to B infift upon his uncle taking a fort of guardianfhip and charge of the plaintiff's wife. The plaintiff and his father, I am told, had been at variance, and the defendant blew the coals. He went down to Scotland, and carried his lady with him, and pretended there had C been great quarrels between her and her hufband, and that it was unfafe for her to accompany him to the Eaft Indies, and that fhe had better remain with the mother. All this while, as I fhall prove, he was carrying on this feduction that gives rife to this caufe. The D defendant's purpofe was carried on for fome time. The niece remained under care of the mother, till fhe (Mrs. Frafer) went to the Eaft Indies to her hufband, and he remained in a connection with this woman, pretending he fhould take care of her as a pa-E rent, during which time he held this inceftuous commerce. As the witneffes come from the other end of the town, I fhall not perhaps be able to begin with that witnefs who is to prove what is very material to this caufe. That before the defendant, the uncle F of this lady, had been three weeks in England, under pretence of going to the father, I fhall be able to prove the defendant was in fuch a fituation with her, as to be able to feduce her; (though I do not afk you to believe it as proof of adultery,) it will be fufficient to G convince you he had caft his eyes upon her at that time, and therefore every thing that happened afterwards, muft be referred to that criminal purpofe which at that time had taken poffeffion of his mind. This was three or four weeks after the plaintiff was at H Hilfea barracks, and it was in that place he firft faw a change in his wife's correfpondence. It was in that place he firft found, but did not know, why her affections

tions were estranged from him, and of which he com- A
plains now; and that her uncle had given directions to
supply her with fine clothes, and accustomed her to
dissipation, which at first seemed to be only the effects
of an indulgent and affectionate parent, but in the end
proved destructive and of bad consequence to him; so B
far was he from imagining that incestuous commerce
took place. My learned friend comes here to main-
tain, that his client is not only innocent of the incestuous
commerce, but that his mind and imagination never
suggested such intercourse. If that is to be set up, it B
never can be suggested that such incestuous commerce
has not in fact taken place. To Captain Campbell it
was difficult to believe it when he heard it, when he
came first from the East Indies. I understand, and I
am extremely glad the cause has not gone off upon ac- D
count of the great distance the witnesses come from.
I have them now in court, they will be called, they
are many in number. I will prove first of all, the defendant was found in a situation with his own niece at
Ramsgate, three weeks after his arrival in England, E
shameful and shocking to relate. I have witnesses that
he was seen almost in the very act of adultery, and that
repeatedly; and if that proof be not sufficient, where
shall we prove it? I shall prove it was his course and
constant habit to sleep with her every night, in the same F
bed, for the whole of the night. It will be suggested
my witnesses come to misrepresent facts—then they
must come with a conspiracy. I should be glad if my
friends will lay the foundation for your belief of it.
The witnesses are persons of character, and some of G
them discharged from places of persons, over whom
my client has no influence; and unless you believe
them to be corrupted with money, to come here to
face God and man, against their conscience to swear
against innocence, you cannot but find a verdict upon H
the facts being proved, which is the object of the action. It is a case of the most serious nature, and must
                                                    depend

A depend upon the complexion that belongs to it, when you have heard both fides. · I fhall lay fuch a cafe before you as I have ftated, and happy fhall I be, as every man muft, if, inftead of ftanding up to fpeak to you again, I fhould fee upon the evidence, he was not **B** guilty, as every man would wifh it not proved againft him ; but I am apprehenfive the evidence is fuch as will urge it upon you, fo far as to deferve your ferious attention and confideration.

———

The Reverend Alexander Clee *fworn.—Examined by* Mr. Mingay.

C
Q. Do you know Mr. Campbell?
A. Yes, I do.
Q. Do you know his wife ? Was you prefent at the marriage ?
A. I married them.
Q. When ?
D
A. On Friday, February 17, 1786—that is the precife day.
Q. Did you know the lady before fhe married ?
A. I did.
Q. Who was fhe ?
E
A. She was a Mifs Frafer.
Q. What relation was fhe to Major Hook ?
A. I underftand they were coufins, that fhe was the daughter of Mrs. Frafer, the wife of Colonel Frafer; and her father was in India at the time.
F
Q. Do you know what relation fhe was to Mrs. Frafer ?
A. I do not.
Q. What age was the lady when fhe married ?
3
A. I can-

A. I cannot fay; fhe was thought to be about feventeen or eighteen.

Examined by Mr. Bearcroft.

Q. You have not faid yet, according to what ceremony they were married ?

A. According to the Church of England mode of marriage, which is ufed at the chapel where I prefide.

Mr. Lawrence Campbell *fworn.—Examined by Mr.* Holroyd.

Q. I believe you know the plaintiff, Captain Campbell ?

A. Yes, Sir.

Q. Were you abroad with Captain Campbell and Mrs Campbell any time ?

A. I was in France with them.

Q. At what time ?

A. In 1787.

Q. Shortly after their marriage ?

A. After their marriage.

Q. I believe Mrs. Campbell, your wife, was with her ?

A. Yes.

Q. Was Mrs. Frafer, Mrs. Campbell's mother with her ?

A. Alfo.

Q. At that time the plaintiff and his wife lived with Mrs. Frafer ?

A. They did, Sir.

Q. Now in what manner did the plaintiff and his wife conduct themfelves to each other ?

A. I always underftood with the greateft harmony.

Lord Chief Juftice. They appeared fo ?

A. They

A A. They appeared ſo.

Q. Mr. *H.* How long were you with them in France?

A. About three weeks.

Q. Were you particularly acquainted with them?

B A. Certainly, Sir, we lived under the ſame roof.

Q. Do you know the defendant?

A. Perfectly well.

Q. Do you know what relation he is to Mrs. Fraſer?

C A. Brother.

Q. And therefore uncle to Mrs. Campbell?

A. Of courſe.

Q. Mr. *Bearcroft.* What relation are you to Mrs. Campbell?

A. I am brother to the plaintiff.

Q. What time in 1787 was it you were in France?

D A. I think it was in the months of July, Auguſt, and September.

Q. There or thereabouts?

A. Yes.

Q. Had you ſeen them together before the time

E they were in France?

A. Not before.

Q. That was the firſt opportunity you had of ſeeing them?

A. I was with Mrs. Fraſer, the mother, in the

F ſame houſe.

Q. You ſaw them daily?

A. I ſaw them daily.

Q. Do you mean to ſay, according to your obſervation, you believed that they lived in perfect har

G mony?

A. Certainly ſo.

Q. You had no reaſon to ſuppoſe the contrary?

A. I had no reaſon to ſuppoſe it.

Q. You never ſaw any thing particular to lead you to it?

A. I.

A. No.   **A**

Q. You never obferved any thing particular in the temper, difpofition, and behaviour of the plaintiff towards his wife?

A. No, Sir.

Q. Did you come home with them?   **B**

A. No, Sir.

Q. Then the only opportunity you had of feeing them together, were thofe two or three months in France?

A. The only time.   **C**

Q. You know the plaintiff's hand writing?

A. Yes, certainly, Sir.

Q. Do me the favour to look at thefe fubfcriptions, and tell me whether they are the plaintiff's?

A. Yes, I do believe that to be his writing.   **D**

Q. Look at that fubfcription?

A. I believe that is.

Q. Do you know what age the lady was when fhe married?

A. I fancy about fifteen or fixteen.   **E**

Q. Juft come from fchool, I believe?

A. Juft come from fchool.

Q. Was Mr. Campbell, the plaintiff, living in the houfe with Mrs. Frafer, the mother, and his wife, at that time?   **F**

A. I underftood fo from him—I cannot fay.

Q. Mr. *Holroyd.* Did you know the lady before fhe was married?

A. Yes, Sir.

Q. Was it a match of inclination—was it a love **G** match?

A. I fhould fuppofe fo.

Q. Mr. *Bearcroft.* Of the parties, moft undoubtedly?

A. I fhould fuppofe fo.   **H**

I   Mr.

A   Q. Mr. *Erskine.*   Pray, Sir, do you know the hand writing of Mrs. Campbell ?

A. No, Sir, I do not.

B   *Mrs.* Campbell *sworn.—Examined by Mr.* Erskine.

Q. You are the wife, I believe, of the gentleman who has just now been examined ?

A. I am the wife of Mr. Campbell.

C   Q. Mr. Lawrence Campbell?

A. Yes, Sir.

Q. Was you acquainted with Mrs. Campbell, the plaintiff's wife ?

A. I was.

D   Q. Did you know her before her marriage ?

A. I did.

Q. Who was she ?

A. She was a Miss Fraser.

Q. How long before this marriage ?

E   A. Two or three years.

Q. Do you remember the courtship between Captain Campbell and her ?

A. No, I do not.

Q. Do you remember her marriage ?

F   A. I heard of it.

Q. Where did you first see her ?

A. In France.

Q. You was there with your husband and Mrs. Fraser ?

G   A. Yes, at Paris, in France, and likewise at Boulogne.

Q. How long ?

A. About a month.

Q. Tell my Lord and the jury, whether you had an

H opportunity of seeing, by living in the manner you described with them, whether Captain Campbell and

his

his wife, Mrs. Campbell, lived in affection with one A
another ?

A. They always appeared to me to be upon very
good terms with one another.

Q. Did they appear so from that sort of circum-
stance a recent marriage from inclination ?   B

A. They did.

Q. You did not keep much company with strangers
in that country ?

A. No, we did not.

Q. Of course lived in each other's company almost C
entirely ?

A. Almost entirely.

Q. Did you ever observe, during that time, any
want of affection from her to him, or he to her ?

A. No, I did not.   D

Q. What age is Captain Campbell, the plaintiff.

A. About thirty.

Q. Do you know Mrs. Campbell's hand writing ?

A. I believe I do.

Q. Look at those letters ?   E

Q. Mr. *Garrow*, You have seen her write ?

A. I have, Sir.

Q. Mr. *Erskine*. Are they her hand writing ?

A. To the best of my knowledge they are.

Mr. *Erskine*. You will cross examine her to that F
if you please.

Mr. *Garrow*. No, we shall not, we might as well
examine Chevalier d'Eon to it.

Another letter shewn her.

Mrs. *C.* I don't know that hand writing.   G

The witness proved several different letters to be her
- hand writing.

I 2   Donald

A Donald Campbell *sworn.—Examined by Mr.* Mingay.

Q. You of courfe know the plaintiff and his wife?
A. I do, Sir.

B Q. Now during the time, from the time they firft came together, till the time when you heard of this unfortunate affair with the family, did they live happy together, or otherwife?
A. They always did.

C Q. Did they affociate much out of their own particular family?
A. I had not an opportunity of feeing much of them, I lived moftly upon the continent; I rather
D think they were moftly living in happinefs together.

Crofs-examined by Mr. Garrow.

E Q. From what time to what time, are you able to give any account of them?
A. From the time of their marriage till I firft heard of this bufinefs.
Q. Where did you fee them, upon the continent?
A. No, I did not, they were in Brook-ftreet, they took lodgings there.
F Q. Was that after they returned from the continent, or before they went?
A. I rather think it was after they returned.
Q. Do you remember what year it was in?
A. I do not recollect.
G Q. I took it for granted you did not, from the manner my friend put his queftion. You cannot tell any year or length of time, from the time of Noah?
Q. *Lord Chief Juftice.* Can you tell about what time?
H A. I cannot. It might be four or five years ago.
Mr.

Q. Mr. *Garrow*. For how long together might you **A**
see them?

A. For a very fhort time, as I mentioned I was
moftly upon the continent.

Q. A very fhort time might mean a month, a week,
or a day? **B**

A. I was about three weeks there, every day almoft, to pay a vifit.

Q. And you an accidental vifitor?
A. Yes, Sir.

Mr. *Bearcroft*. The defendant returned to Eng- **C**
land about February 7, 1788, as appears by my
brief.

Elizabeth Herbfon *fworn.—Examined by Mr.* Holroyd. **D**

Q. I believe you lived as cook with Mrs. Frafer?
A. I did.

Q. Were you in that capacity with her in the year
1788? **E**

A. Yes, Sir, I was.

Q. Do you remember the family going to Ramfgate in the year 1788?

A. Yes, Sir, I do.

Q. How long was that after Major Hook's arrival? **F**
Do you remember in what month?

A. I believe it was in July.

Q. Mrs. Frafer went to Ramfgate?
A. Yes.

Q. And Mrs. Campbell? **G**
A. Yes.

Q. Was Major Hook there?
A. He was not.

Q. He came there after you went?
A. Yes, he did. **H**

Q. Where was Captain Campbell?
A. I believe at Chatham, or Portfmouth.

Q. Was

A Q. Was he with his regiment there ?

A. I cannot say.

Q. How long was they at Ramfgate ?

A. I believe ten weeks.

Q. Do you remember feeing any thing particular

B between Mrs. Campbell and Major Hook ?

A. Never but once, Sir, when I went in with a bit of bread.

Q. When you went in where ?

A. To the parlour.

C Q. What did you fee there ?

A. I faw the Major fitting with his arm round her neck, and his right leg upon her lap.

Q. Did you obferve any thing refpecting her hair ?

A. Yes, Sir, her hair was rolled round his arm.

D Q. State what you faw.

A. Her hair was rolled round his left arm.

Q. Did you obferve any thing farther ?

A. His right hand in her handkerchief.

Lord Chief Juftice.   Q. The handkerchief that co-

E vered her neck ?

A. Yes.

Counfel.   Q. Did you obferve any thing elfe ?

A. No, Sir, I did not.

Q. Do you remember Major Hook's arrival at

F Ramfgate?

A. Yes, I do.

Q. Did any thing particular pafs at the time ?

A. Mrs. Campbell was very much alarmed, and fainted away upon his coming in ; I remember that,

G Sir.

Q. That you remember ?

A. Yes, Sir.

Lord Chief Juftice.   Q. At who's coming there ?

A. At Major Hook's, the defendant's.

H   *Counfel.*   Q. Where did they return again from Ramfgate ?

A. To

A. To Brook-ftreet. **A**

Q. To Mis. Frafer's ?

A. Yes, to the houfe they came from.

Q. Did they all come together ?

A. No, I believe the Major went to his houfe.

Q. You returned ? **B**

A. Yes.

Q. To Brook-ftreet, Mrs. Frafer's houfe ?

A. Yes.

Q. Major Hook went to his own houfe ?

A. Yes. **C**

Q. What time was it you faw that at Ramfgate you have been defcribing ?

A. It was fome time in the morning.

Q. In what month ?

A. I cannot fay. **D**

Q. You faid you went there in July ?

A. Yes, I think it was about Michaelmas time.

Q. How long was it before you returned to town ?

A. We came to town fome time in September.

E

Crofs-examined by Mr. Bearcroft.

Q. What was your fituation in the family ?

A. Cook. **F**

Q. You went by order to the parlour ?

A. No, I went to carry a bit of bread, by Mrs. Frafer's order.

Q. For whom ?

A. For Mrs. Campbell and Major Hook.

Q. They took it, as if they expected it ? **G**

A. I do not know whether they expected it or not.

Q. You carried it, and you gave it them ?

A. I did not look at them when I gave the plate.

Q. You went for the purpofe of carrying the bread **H** there, and it was received ?

A. Yes.

A A. Yes.

Q. No body faid for what it was fent?

A. No.

Q. It was expected therefore?

A. Yes.

B Q. The door was open when you went in?

A. Yes, Sir, it was.

Q. Was it wide open?

A. Partly open.

Q. You delivered the bread and went away; you

C did not ftay, I fuppofe?

A. I did not ftop a moment hardly.

Q. You ftepp'd in, and delivered the bread, and went away?

A. Yes.

D Q. You did not ftop at all?

A. No.

Q. You did not let the plate fall?

A. No, I held it fo, and one of them took it, I don't know which.

E [The witnefs held out her hand with the bread one way, and turned her face the other way.]

Q. You did not exprefs any particular furprife?

A. Why, Sir, I cannot fay I liked to fee them fo.

Q. You made all thefe obfervations?

F A. Yes.

Q. Of courfe you thought it extremely improper?

A. Very, Sir.

Q. Did you ever fee Mr. Campbell, the hufband, after that?

G A. I believe I did fee him once—he came in the hall once. I don't recollect I ever faw him but once after that.

Q. I take it for granted you told Mrs. Frafer, the mother, immediately?

A. No, I did not, Sir.

H Mr. *Holroyd.* How came you to take the bread up?

A. Mrs.

A. Mrs. Frafer ordered me to carry the bread. **A**
Lord Chief Juftice. She faid fo before.
Q. Where was Mrs. Frafer?
A. She was in one parlour, and the Major and Mrs. Campbell in the other.

B

Robert Green called and appeared.

Jofeph Rippington *fworn.—Examined by Mr. Er-* **C**
fkine.

Q. Did you live, Sir, at any time with Mr. Hook, the defendant?
A. Yes, Sir, I did.
Q. In what capacity did you live with him? **D**
A. I was hired to him as a valet.
Q. At what time?
A. In the year 1789.
Q. At what time of the year?
A. In the beginning of May. **E**
[*Green was ordered to withdraw, on motion of defendant's counfel.*]
Q. Do you *know the witnefs* that is juft now retired out of court?
A. I faw him after I left the Major, but while I **F** lived there, I have feen him.
Q. Did you live there before him?
A. Before him.
Q. You came there in May 1789?
A. Yes. **G**
Q. Where was your mafter living at that time?
A. At the Bath Hotel.
Q. Was he living at the Bath Hotel, when you lived with him?
A. Yes, he was; he had been there fome time. **H**
Q. That was his place of refidence?
A. Yes.

K Q. Who

A   Q. Who lived with him there ?

A. There was a lady living with him there, that I underſtood to be Mrs. Campbell.

Q. Do you know now who it was ? did you ever hear the defendant ſay who it was ?

B   A. No, Sir, not the defendant, only by calling her by the name of Mrs. Campbell.

Q. You heard the defendant call her Mrs. Campbell ?

A. Yes, every time almoſt that I went into the
C room.

Q. How long did you continue at the Bath Hotel ?

A. I continued about three weeks.

Q. Where did your maſter go from the Bath Hotel ?

D   A. He went into Sackville-ſtreet.

Q. How long did you continue there ?

A. About two months.

Q. Be ſo good as to tell me whether, when he was living in Sackville-ſtreet, the defendant gave you di-
E rections to buy any thing, and what ?

A. He deſired I would buy ſome prints.

Q. Of what ſort ?

A. He ſaid ſmutty ones, the moſt ſmutty ones I could get.

F   Q. Did you in conſequence of theſe directions buy any ?

A. Yes, Sir, I did.

Q. Did he tell you what he wanted them for ?

A. He told me he wanted to ſend them to India, to
G a friend in India.

Q. Did he tell you where to find them ?

A. No, Sir, he did not know where.

Q. Did you buy them ?

A. Yes, I did.

H   Q. They are of a nature I ſhould think it very ſhameful to exhibit in the court ?

A. They are.

Lord

Lord Chief Justice. I am very sorry there is a market to be found for those things. **A**

Mr. *Bearcroft.* It is a pity but it should be known, that the Attorney General may hear of it.

Mr. *Erskine.* Q. Are they prints of the most indecent nature? **B**

A. Yes, they are the most so that I could get.

Q. Did you ever see any of those prints that you purchased for Major Hook, in the Major's hand, and and upon what occasion?

A. I went into the room one day. **C**

Q. Did he expect you at the time you went in?

A. No, Sir, he did not.

Q. You went into the room at a time he did not expect you, with a message? Tell us what was in the room when you came in. **D**

A. There was Mrs. Campbell and the Major.

Q. Now be so good to tell us what you saw?

A. He had one of those prints in his hand I had been purchasing for him, and she was looking over his shoulder. **E**

Lord Chief Justice. Q. She was looking over his shoulder at the prints?

A. Yes, Sir; when I came in, she turned her head, and walked away towards the window.

Q. Now, Sir, I ask you, upon your solemn oath, **F** whether you are now relating what you positively know?

A. Yes, Sir; I do, Sir; I know it to be a fact.

Q. Now, Sir, in consequence, of your having seen this, did it occur to you to have a suspicion of connection? **G**

Mr. *Garrow.* Suspicion—is that a question?

Mr. *Erskine.* I think your objection is valid, and will not continue it. Where was Major Hook and Mrs. Campbell's apartments in Sackville-street? **H**

A. Their bed-rooms adjoined one another.

K 2   Q. Major

A   Q. Major Hook's bed-chamber and Mrs. Campbell's joined together?

A. Mrs. Campbell's and Major Hook's joined to one another.

B   Q. Was there any opening between one room and the other?

A. Yes, there was a door that went out of one room into the other.

Q. Did you ever travel with Mr. Hook and Mrs. Campbell?

C   A. Yes, Sir, I did all the summer.

Q. To what parts did you travel?

A. Travelled all through South Wales.

Q. Did any body accompany them?

A. Nobody at all, no other servant but myself.

D   Q. No other person but the defendant and Mrs. Campbell?

A. No, Sir, nobody.

Q. Be so good as to tell us whether you remember any particular direction given by the defendant, in the

E   course of your journey, at any particular inn?

A. When he went to take any lodgings in town, he would not take them unless there were two bedrooms communicating with one another; and it was so at all the inns; if not so, he would not stop, but go

F   to another inn.

Q. Was this in particular, or in general only?

A. It was in general, at all the places that ever I saw?

Q. Do you know what time Captain Campbell

G   went to India?

A. No, I do not.

Q. *(To Mr. Hawkins, attorney for the plaintiff).* What time did he go?

Mr. *Hawkins.* A. He went on board, December

H   1788, and sailed in the beginning of January, 1789.

Q. *(To the witness.)* Did you ever see, besides that

print

print Mrs. Campbell was looking at, any publication **A** laying in the room ?

A. Yes, I did fee a book of a divorcement.

Q. What book was it ?

A. It was either the Marchionefs of Carmarthen, or Lady Tyrconnel.

Q. The trial ? **B**

A. The trial.

Q. Did you fee it laying open ?

A. Yes, I faw it laying in the drawing-room.

Q. The drawing-room where the defendant and Mrs. Campbell lived ?

A. The very room, Sir.

Q. Have you ever had any opportunity ?

[*Here Mr. Garrow objected to the leading quef-tion.*] **C**

As I don't wifh to lead you.—Do you know any thing elfe material to inform the court—any thing that you obferved particular between Mrs. Campbell and the defendant ?

A. When I was at the Ivy Bufh at Carmarthen, they **D** had two rooms, one behind the other. Mrs. Camp-bell fleeped in the other one.

Lord Chief Juftice. Q. Did you obferve any thing there ?

A. No, my Lord, I did not, only from the cham- **E** ber-maids, what they told me.

Robert Green *fworn.*—*Examined by Mr.* Mingay.

F

Q. Did you at any time live with Mr. Hook ?

A. I did.

Q. When ?

A. In the year 1790.

Q. Did you go in 1789, or 1790 ?

A. 1790, Sir. **G.**

Q. Do

A   Q. Do you know whether at that time Captain Campbell was abroad ?

A. He was abroad.

Q. Where was it firſt of all you lived with Major Hook ?

B   A. In Duke-ſtreet, Mancheſter-ſquare.

Q. Do you remember going into the drawing-room, and ſeeing any thing particular between Mr. Hook and Mrs. Campbell ?

A. I had been in Major Hook's ſervice about ſix C weeks and a day or two; but before that, I had a ſuſpicion from what I had ſeen between Major Hook and Mrs. Campbell, I thought there was ſomething going on improper between an uncle and niece. After dinner, more from curioſity than any thing elſe, I went D up into the drawing-room, and I ſaw Major Hook and Mrs. Campbell ſitting on the couch, which ſtood behind the door, in a very criminal way, with one arm round Mrs. Campbell's neck, and the other under her petticoats; I plainly could ſee Mrs. Campbell's E knee.

Q. Her naked knee?

A. Her naked knee.

Q. Did you go out of town with Mr. Hook and Mrs. Campbell ?

F   A. Yes.—After this, one day, Major Hook ſays to Mrs. Campbell, I am going out now, and I will come in to dinner.—I remember we had for dinner a cod's head and ſounds, and Major Hook never came in to dinner. Mrs. Campbell waited very impatiently till G ſix o'clock, when ſhe ſeemed in a violent paſſion, and ordered me to take the dinner down, and ſhe would not eat any dinner. She ſeemed very much enraged to think he did not come home to dinner; with that he came home, about half paſt ten at night. When he H came home, I let him in; he went up into the drawing-room, I went down into the kitchen. When I had been down there the courſe of a quarter of an

hour,

hour, I heard a violent scream, and a cry of murder; **A**
with that I went up into the drawing-room, and I perceived Major Hook standing in a corner of the room,
with a chair before him, and she trying to strike him
with a poker; with that he desired me to quit the
room, which I did; I went down into the kitchen. I **B**
had not been there above five minutes, when I heard a
violent crying out again, and Mrs. Campbell run down
stairs; this was about half past eleven, or near twelve:
she ran out into the street, Major Hook followed her,
and desired me to go after her, which I did; I fol- **B**
lowed her out, and I overtook her a little way down
Duke-street: she was in a deplorable condition, her
handkerchief tore all off her neck, and Major Hook
with waistcoat tore open, and down as far as here.

[*Pointing to about three inches from the waist.*] **D**
With that I said, says I, for God's sake Mrs. Campbell come in.

Q. Did she come in?

A. I followed her, and overtook her, and said, for
God's sake Mrs. Campbell come in, consider what **E**
condition you are in, and the time of night, and
you will be taken up by the watch, and put in the
watch-house, with that she returned, and shut herself
in the parlour.

Q. Did any thing else happen? **F**

A. She shut herself in the parlour, and Major Hook
came and said, Harriet, Harriet, I insist upon your
coming out, I pray you to come out; she came out,
and was running up stairs, her foot slipp'd, and she
fell down upon the landing place, she fainted away, **G**
or pretended it, with that Major Hook stood over her,
and proclaimed these words: " You are a whore, a
" d—d whore, and you are the worst of whores.—
She replied, " I am a whore, but it is only to you,
" who ought to have been my father, my friend, my **H**
" protector; instead of that, you have been my utter
" ruin, and my friends. Oh my poor husband !"

Q. Repeat

A   Q. Repeat it again?

A. He said, " you are a whore, you are a d—d " whore, you are the worst of whores."—She said, " I " am a whore, I own, but to you only, you ought to " have been my father, and protector, and friend, in-
B " stead of that you have been my entire ruin, and my " friends. Oh my poor husband!"

Q. Do you remember any thing while Mrs. Campbell and Mr. Hook lived in Duke-street, having seen what passed before, having the curiosity of going to
C her bed-room?

A. I had.

Q. When?

A. There was a person living there, one Betty White, a servant to Mr. Whitehouse, in Duke-street,
D she came down and joked with me, and said, come here, and look at the bed, I said, by G—d, here has been more than one in the bed to-night, for when I went up, I perceived the print of two people in the bed.

E   Q. In Mrs. Campbell's bed?

A. In Mrs. Campbell's bed.

Q. Do you recollect going to Swansea with Mr. Hook and Mrs. Campbell?

A. Perfectly well.

F   Q. When was that?

A. In 1790, or 1791, I don't know which.

Q. Do you remember passing through the bed-room—what observation did you make?

A. I recollect Major Hook always took care, where-
G ever we went, to whatever lodgings, to have two rooms communicating with each other.

Q. Do you remember, while at Swansea, going to a room adjoining to her bed-chamber?

A. I do, it was one day after dinner, I was in the
H court-yard with the children, and Major Hook's son said I was wanted; I went up stairs.

2

Q. Did

Q. Did you go into the room adjoining, where **A**
Major Hook and Mrs. Campbell were?

A. Yes, I went into the room, and I perceived that
Major Hook and Mrs. Campbell were laying at the
foot of the bed.

Q. Was it in her bed-room? **B**

A. In her bed-room, and on the bed; as soon as
they saw me, it put them in a surprize, he started up,
and the flap of his breeches hung down, and his face
was as red as fire; the colour came all up into his
face, and Mrs. Campbell walked to another part of the **C**
room.

Q. At that time did you observe any part of the
person of Mrs. Campbell?

A. Yes, I did—I saw at that time up as far as here,
(pointing to the knee.) **D**

Q. Her thighs?

A. Yes, I did.

Q. Her naked thighs?

A. Her naked thighs. Then we went from Walton, and took a house at Twickenham. I left them **E**
at Twickenham. That is all I know.

Cross-examined by Mr. Garrow.
F

Q. Pray, Mr. Green, how long did you live in the
service of Major Hook?

A. About eleven months.

Q. Did your wife live there?

A. I was married when I lived with Major Hook, **G**
and he asked for my wife to go down to Swansea, to
attend the children; she was there about six weeks;
she was a weekly servant.

Q. Were you at last discharged without warning?

A. I gave him warning frequently. **H**

Q. Was you at last discharged without warning?

A. I was, Major Hook undermined me, and hired

L   another

A another fervant, before he let me know his intention.

    Q. After, you fay, you giving him warning fre-
quently, had paffed by you, and you continued?

    A. Yes.

B   Q. The warning was not exifting at the time you
were difcharged?

    A. Yes, it was.

    Q. How long had you given warning before?

    A. Several times.

C   Q. He undermined you?

    A. Yes.

    Q. And did it unhandfomely?

    A. Yes.

    Q. You have frequently expreffed yourfelf fo, that
D he had ufed you extremely ill?

    A. No.

    Q. That you have frequently expreffed?

    A. That I never expreffed.

    Q. To no perfon upon earth?

E   A. No.

    Q. You never complained Major Hook ufed you
ill?

    A. I cannot fay but I may have faid he did not ufe
me well; I never heard he ufed any fervant well.

F   Q. This gentleman never ufed any body well?

    A. I heard he never did, not as a fervant.

    Q. Your reafons for going to look at Mrs. Camp-
bell's bed were, that Betty White invited you there?

    A. Yes, frequently.

G   Q. You have ftated you faw the impreffion of two
perfons having lain upon the bed?

    A. Yes, Mrs. Campbell's bed.

    Q. Did you obferve any thing elfe particular?

    A. Yes,

H   Q. Perhaps Betty White fhew'd it you?

    A. No.

    Q. It was in her prefence you faw it?

    A. She

A   She was in another part of the room.   A

Q. Did you communicate it to her?

A. No, I did not like to do so to a woman.

Q. Not to a woman that desired you to observe two
people had lain in the bed?

No answer.   B

Q. You said she was a servant to a person of the
name of Whitehouse?

A. She was; Mr. Whitehouse certainly has heard
me mention it.

Q. About that time?   C

A. About that time.

Q. How often might Betty White invite you to
look at the bed?

A. Upon my word I cannot tell, I did not take
any particular notice of it.   D

Q. It happened frequently?

A. Frequently.

Q. Perhaps two or three dozen times?

A. No, but very frequently.

Sarah Green *sworn.*—*Examined by Mr.* Holroyd,

Q. You are wife to the last witness?   E

A. I am, Sir.

Q. Did you live with Mr. Hook and Mrs. Campbell?

A. I was not a hired servant, but I was with them
about the course of six weeks.   F

Q. Did you go with them to Swansea?

A. Yes, I did.

Q. When was that?

A. In the year 1791.

Q. When they were at Swansea, how were their bed-   G
rooms situate?

A. They were all upon a floor, there were three
upon

A upon the floor. The Major had one, Mrs. Campbell had the other, and the children the other.

Q. Was there any communications between Mr. Hook's and Mrs. Campbell's?

B A. Yes, Sir, the children's room was between them.

Lord Chief Justice. Q. Did the rooms immediately communicate, or was the children's room between them?

C A. The children's room was between them.

Lord Chief Justice. Q. The other man said they opened one to the other?

A. They were so, the doors that communicated D with the children's room, was between them, but the doors all opened to communicate to the other rooms.

Q. Was there any communication from Mrs. Campbell's room to Mr. Hook's, except through the children's room?

E A. No, Sir.

Q. Did the children always sleep in the room?

A. Yes, mostly; sometimes the oldest son slept with the father—sometimes, though not always.

Jury. Q. Were those Mrs. Campbell's children?

A. No, Sir, they were Major Hook's children.

F Mr. *Holroyd.* Q. How many children had Mr. Hook?

A. Three, Sir, two girls and a boy.

Q. Do you recollect any particular directions given at the inns where they came to?

G A. No, I cannot.

Q. How were the rooms?

A. Always joining together; they always refused to take rooms, except they joined. I remember when they were at the next inn to Swansea, they would not H take the rooms, because they were not adjoining, if they *travelled all night.*

Q. The apartments for themselves and children, all joined together.

A. Yes,

A. Yes, fometimes the children ufed to fleep with **A** her—when there might be two beds in a room, the children ufed to fleep in one, and Mrs. Campbell in the other.

Q. Who attended the children?

A. I always attended the children. **B**

Q. Did you fleep with them?

A. No, I ufed to fleep up ftairs in a room juft directly above them.

Q. About what age might they be?

A. I fhould fuppofe the eldeft fon was about eleven **C** or twelve years of age, the others younger.

Q. Who attended Mrs. Campbell when fhe went to bed?

A. I always attended her.

Q. You left her of courfe when fhe went to bed? **D**

A. Yes, Sir.

Q. How was the door left?

A. Always open; fhe always defired me to leave the door of her own room, and the door of the children's room open, both. **E**

Mr. *Mingay*. Q. Do you mean the door of the paffage?

A. Yes, Sir, that which opened to go into the immediate room, next that which opened to her room. **F**

Mr. *Garrow*. Q. And went off the ftair-cafe into the room?

A. Yes.

Q. Did you leave that door open?

A. Yes, Sir, I did. **G**

Q. You went out of the ftair-cafe into the room?

A. Yes.

Q. Whofe room?

A. The children's room on one fide, and the lady's on the other. **H**

Q. Was there any way into Mrs. Campbell's, but thorough the children's room?

A. No,

A   A. No, Sir, not at Swansea.

Q. When you were in Mrs. Campbell's, has any body come into the room?

A. Yes, the Major has frequently come into the room before I left it.

B   Q. And Mrs. Campbell quite naked?

A. Almoſt undreſſed, and he half undreſſed.

Q. Did he ſee you there?

A. Yes, Sir, he did, and when he ſaw me there, he uſed to return again to his own room.

C   Q. Has that been once, or oftener?

A. Why, Sir, oftener.

Q. Where was this at, Swanſea?

A. *Yes, Sir, at Swanſea*, during the courſe of the time I was there.

D   Q. *Have you obſerved any thing about the bed?*

A. No, Sir, I never did obſerve it.

Q. *Did you make the bed, or the maid of the houſe make it?*

A. Why, ſometimes I, and ſometimes the maid of **E** the houſe, it was not a particular rule for either.

Croſs-examined by Mr. Bearcroft.

F   Q. What time of the year was it you were at Swanſea?

A. Why, I went about the middle of June; and came home about the latter end of Auguſt.

Q. You occaſionally, perhaps, helped to make the **G** bed?

A. I did, Sir.

Q. You made no obſervation upon it?

A. I never did, Sir; I never noticed it.

Q. Your huſband never made the bed?

H   A. No, Sir.

Q. Did you go away when your huſband did?

A. Yes;

A. Yes, Sir, I did.   A

Q. Was you turned away ?

A. No, Sir, I was not.

Q. You went away, becaufe he went way ?

A. No, I went away on the Friday ; they faid they
would take me back again, and my hufband was not B
willing I fhould go.

Q. Your hufband was ill-ufed, you thought ?

A. No farther than they had words ; my hufband
did not wifh me to go back, as I was not in a fituation
for fervice.   C

Robert Green *called again.*

Lord Chief Juſtice.   Q. You fay orders were given D
in the courfe of your journey, the apartments fhould
be together ?

A. He never gave me any other orders about the
apartments, but that I fhould always take care to
have his apartments together.   E

Q. His family, that travelled with him, were this
lady, his niece, and the children ?

A. Yes.

Q. How many apartments did they confift of ?

A. *He chofe to have two adjoining rooms, and the* F
doors communicating with each other.   There were three
rooms on the floor at Swanfea where we lodged : Major
Hook's was on the left, here was the children's, and
here Mrs. Campbell's *(defcribing them by motion of*
his hand) at Swanfea ?   G

Q. Was there any immediate communication at
Swanfea between Mrs. Campbell's and the Major's ?

A. The children's room parted them.

Elizabeth

Elizabeth Hern *fworn.—Examined by Mr.* Erſkine.

A   Q. Did you live at any time with Mr. Hook?

A. Yes, Sir, I did.

Q. When did you go to him?

A. I lived with Mrs. Fraſer firſt.

Q. How long did you live in the whole with Mrs.
B Fraſer—did you live with Mr. Hook afterwards?

A. Yes, when he came up to London.

Q. Was you ſervant to Mr. Hook, or only ſervant
to Mrs. Fraſer?

A. Servant to Mrs. Fraſer.

C   Q. When did you go to live with her?

A. In February.

Q. In what year?

A. In February 1788.

Q. Where did Mrs. Fraſer live?

D   A. Mrs. Fraſer lived in Brook-ſtreet.

Q. Did Mr. Hook live there?

A. Yes, Sir, a good while.

Q. How long did you continue to live as ſervant
with Mrs. Fraſer?

E   A. I was Mrs. Fraſer's ſervant the whole time.

Q. Had ſhe any houſe any where elſe except in
Brook-ſtreet?

A. Yes, at Walton upon Thames.

Q. Did Mr. Hook come there occaſionally?

F   A. Yes, Sir.

Q. Did you at any time obſerve any thing particular
paſs between the defendant and the wife of the plaintiff?

A. Never but once.

Q. Will you ſtate to my Lord and the Jury what
G that was—where it was?

A. At Walton.

Q. In what year?

A. In

A. In 1788.

A

Q. Do you remember in what month ?

A. I think it was in November.

Q. You are not particular as to time—what did you fee ?

A. I faw Major Hook go into Mrs. Campbell's B room, between ten and eleven o'clock ni the evening.

Q. How came you to be in a fituation to fee hat ?

A. I had the curiofity to watch.   C

Q. Why had you the curiofity to watch ?

A. Becaufe I thought I had heard him go into the room before.

Q. And where did you ftand ?

A. I ftaid upon the landing place.   D

Q. In what drefs was he ?

A. Only in his fhirt and night-cap.

Q. Do you know whether Mrs. Campbell was in her room at the time ?

A. Yes, Sir.   E

Q. Who had attended her to bed ?

A. I, Sir.

Q. Do you know whether the door was fhut or open ?

A. No, Sir, it was left a jar.   F

Q. Do you know why it was left a jar ?

A. Yes, becaufe fhe told me to leave it fo.

Q. Had you left it fo at other times by her directions ?

A. Yes, I have.   G

Q. Were the family gone to bed at that time ?

A. There was nobody in the houfe but the Major and I, and the fervant, and Mrs. Campbell.

Q Yourfelf, and the Major, and Mrs. Campbell, and the man fervant ?   H

A. Except the gardener and his family.

M   Q. You

A   Q. You from fufpicion of courfe watched ?
A. Yes.
Q. Was his head covered ?
A. He had his night-cap on.
Q. Did you fee him go into the room ?
B   A. Yes, I did.
Q. Was the door fhut afterwards ?
A. Yes.
Q. How long did you wait ?
A. I did not wait at all there, I went down imme-
C diately.
Q. Was Mrs. Campbell in bed, or up, at that
time ?
A. She was in bed.
Q. Did you go to bed immediately after that ?
D   A. Yes, I did.
Q. Did you fee the bed in the morning ?
A. Yes, Sir;
Q. Did you attend Mrs. Campbell in the morning
before fhe was up ?
E   A. Yes, Sir.
Q. Did you fee her rife ?
A. Yes.
Q. Had you an opportunity of feeing the bed before
any body elfe came into the room ?
F   A. I, myfelf, made the bed.
Q. Did you fee it as fhe rofe from it, without being
touched by any body elfe ?
A. I cannot fay that, Sir.
Q. Except the Major, Mrs. Campbell, and you,
G *you fay there was none in the houfe but the fervant, the
gardener, and his family ?*
A. No, Sir.
Q. You made the bed upon her getting up ?
A. Yes.
H   Q. How did it appear to you ?
A. *It appeared to me as if more than one flept in it.*
Q. You .

Q. You saw him go into the room, and the door **A**
was left a jar—you saw him go in his shirt and his
night-cap?

A. Yes.

Q. Is there any thing else you can communicate to
the court? **B**

A. No.

Q. Where do you live now—in what service?

A. I don't live in service, I am in business for
myself.

Q. Whose servant was you at the time? **C**

A. Mrs. Fraser's.

Q. Where was Mrs. Fraser at that time?

A. Mrs. Fraser was not at Walton.

Q. Did you tell any body else of it?

A. There was a woman with me. **D**

Cross-examined by Mr. Bearcroft.

Q. You was Mrs. Fraser's servant? **E**

A. Yes.

Q. When you lived at Walton, Mrs. Fraser had
quitted her house in Brook-street?

A. Yes, she did.

Q. Do you mean to say it was in the year 1788? **F**

A. To the best of my knowledge.

Q. We are now in the year 1793—how long was
it ago—was it after Captain Campbell went abroad?

A. I lived with them at the time he went abroad.

Q. Did you ever see Captain Campbell there? **G**

A. I have seen him at Walton.

Q. Leaving the time to shift for itself, are you positive of what you saw?

A. Yes, I am, Sir.

Q. Mr. *Erskine.* What business are you in for **H**
yourself?

A. In the public line.

M 2   Q. What

A Q. What room did Mr. Hook sleep in at Walton?
A. Next to Mrs. Campbell's.
Q. She desired you to leave the room door a jar?
A. Yes.
Q. Do you know whether Major Hook's was so?
B A. I don't know.

Andrew Addison *called.*

The oath being tendered, he was observed not to
C kiss the book. Upon which Lord Kenyon said, ad-
minister the oath to him again—what is the meaning
he will not kiss the book?
The oath re-administered.
Lord Chief Justice. Now kiss the book.
D The witness then kissed the book, and said, I never
was in a court before to give evidence.
Mr. *Mingay.* Q. Now you are upon oath—
had you any intention to avoid kissing the book, upon
your oath?
E A. Upon my oath I had not.
Lord Chief Justice. If I was upon oath, I should
say, I believe I had.
Mr. *Erskine.* Then I certainly will not call a
witness that my Lord makes such an observation upon.

F   Arabella Kenedy *sworn.*

Q. Did you live at Walton?
A. Yes, Sir.
Q. Did you live servant with Mrs. Fraser?
A. Yes.
G Q. Where do you live now?
A. I live now with my friends.
Q. Do you know Mr. Hook, the defendant?
A. Yes, Sir.
Q. How long did you live at Walton, with Mrs.
Fraser?
                                        A. I

A. I went to Mrs. Fraser in the year 1790, or **A**
1791, I think.

Q. We are now only in 1793, how long is it ago?

A. It is two years next April fince I left her.

Q. When did you go to her—and how long did
you live with her? **B**

A. About eighteen months.

Q. And it is two years next April fince you went
away?

A. Yes.

Q. Do you remember Mrs. Campbell being there? **C**

A. Yes.

Q. And Mr. Hook being there?

A. Yes, Sir.

Q. How far were their rooms apart—how were
they fituated?

A. *They were next adjoining each other.* **D**

Q. In what capacity was you there?

A. Sometimes cook, and fometimes houfe-maid.

Q. Did you fee at any time, and when, any thing
particular between Mr. Hook and Mrs. Campbell?

A. At one time, at Mrs. Fraser's, I faw them ftand-
up near each other, and Mrs. Campbell's hand in **E**
Major Hook's hand.

Q. Did you fee any thing elfe then?

A. No, Sir.

Q. Did you fee any thing elfe at Walton?

A. One night I faw Mrs. Campbell's room door **F**
open, and Mr. Hook went into her room, after fhe
had retired to bed

Q. In what drefs?

A. *He had at that time all his cloaths on but his
hat.* **G**

Q. What time was that?

A. It was after the children were in bed.

Q. Did you fee him come out?

A. No.

Q. Had

A   Q. Had you an opportunity at Walton to see the bed Mrs. Campbell laid in ?

A. Yes, I made it generally.

Q. Did you ever make any obfervation upon the bed, when you made it ?

B   A. No, Sir.

Crofs-examined by Mr. Bearcroft.

C   Q. His cloaths were on, you fay ?

A. Yes, Sir.

Q. Do you know whether Mrs. Campbell was ill at that time ?

A. No, Sir, fhe was not ill at that time.

Q. I want to know whether it did not happen fre-
D quently at Walton, that Mrs. Campbell was ill, and in violent fits of paffion ?

A. Yes, Sir, I have been informed fo, but I never was prefent at any of thofe fits.

Q. Have you ever remembered her having fits in
E town ?

A. No, Sir.

James Woodroffe *fworn.*—*Examined by Mr.* Mingay.

F   Q. What are you ?

A. A gardener, Sir.

Q. Did you live at any time with Mrs. Frafer ?

A. Yes, Sir.

Q. The mother of Mrs. Campbell ?

A. Yes, Sir.

G   Q. Where did fhe live ?

A. At Walton.

Q. Was that after Mr. Campbell, her hufband, was gone abroad ?

A. Yes, it was after Captain Campbell went abroad.

Q. Was fhe with her mother then ?

A. Yes.

A. Yes. **A**

Q. Do you remember any time when Mrs. Fraser was not at her houſe at Walton, Mrs. Campbell and Mr. Hook coming there?

A. Yes, Mr. Hook had taken the houſe.

Q. Mrs. Fraser was not there when they went to **B** look at it?

A. No, Sir.

Q. What obſervation did you make of the conduct of Mr. Hook and Mrs. Campbell?

A. I don't know, Sir, I thought they were very **C** loving.

Q. What did you ſee?

A. I ſaw him between his own room and her's, Sir, in his ſhirt and night-cap.

Q. Where was he coming to or from? **D**

A. From her bed-room; it appeared to me it was between her room and his, in the paſſage, in his ſhirt and night-cap. I did not perceive any thing elſe.

Q. Who was in the houſe at that time?

A. There was my wife, and a nurſe, and me, and **E** *Betty Hearn.*

Q. At that time the mother was not there?

A. No, Sir.

No Croſs-examination.

William Lewis *ſworn.—Examined by Mr.* Holroyd.

Q. You were groom to Major Hook? **F**

A. Yes, Sir.

Q. What time did you go to him?

A. About Auguſt, in the year 1790.

Q. How long did you live with him?

A. I lived with him about ten months. **G**

Q. Did you go with Major Hook and Mrs. Campbell to Swanſea?

A. I

A   A. I was hired by Major Hook in Carmarthenfhire, and went from thence with him to Swanfea.

Q. Do you remember how the bed-rooms were at the inn at Swanfea ?

A. I was not there, they were lodgings.

B   *Lord Chief Juſtice.* It is pretty well afcertained that the bed-rooms adjoined together.

Mr. *Mingay.* My Lord, I muſt beg leave to ſtate to your Lordſhip, with refpect to Andrew Addifon, he came to prove no fact at all in the caufe, but when **C** Captain Campbell left England, and when he returned.

Lord Chief Juſtice. I obferved nothing more about him than my perfonal obfervation, merely as to not kiffing the book ; it raifed fufpicion.

D   Mr. *Mingay.* It was only to prove that Captain Campbell went abroad in the beginning of 1789.

Mr. *Garrow.* In point of fact, he failed from Torbay on the 26th or 27th of January, 1789, and went on board in December 1788.

E   Mr. *Mingay.* And he did not return till 1792.

Mr. *Bearcroft* admitted it.

Q. To *William Lewis.* Whilft you were living with Major Hook, did you make any obfervations on Mrs. Campbell ?

F   A. When I went there, I did not know but they were fingle ; when I came to Swanfea, Mrs. Campbell was with Major Hook, I inquired, and found fhe was his niece.

Q. You remember his coming from Swanfea ?

G   A. Yes, Sir.

Jane Grimes *ſworn.—Examined by Mr.* Erſkine.

H   Q. Did you live in the fervice of the defendant any time, and when ?

A. I lived with Major Hook five months.

I   Q. In

Q. In 1792, was it? **A**

A. Yes.

Q. You lived there as cook?

A. Yes.

Q. Did Mrs. Campbell live with him at that time? **B**

A. Yes.

Q. Did any body elfe live with him?

A. No, Sir.

Q. How long did you continue in his fervice? **C**

A. Five months.

Q. Did you go to Eaft Bourne with him?

A. Yes.

Q. Was Captain Campbell gone abroad then?

A. Yes.

Q. During that time whether you faw any thing **D** particular in the conduct of Mrs. Campbell and Major Hook?

A. What I faw was when I went up ftairs when the grocer came to fpeak to my miftrefs, I went to her room and rapped at the door and fhe was not there; **E** I went from thence, and was coming by the Major's door and I found it fhut.

Q. How was the Major's room fituated in refpect to her's?

A. Almoft clofe. **F**

Q. Were the doors next to each other?

A. They went out of one into the other.

Q. Was it fhut?

A. I tried it.

Q. Was it upon the fpring or locked? **G**

A. I tried it and it was faft.

Q. What did you do then?

A. I had the curiofity to look through the key-hole.

Q. Tell my Lord what was your reafon for look- **H** ing through the key-hole.

A. Becaufe I thought Mrs. Campbell was there:

N Q. What

A   Q. What was your reason for thinking so?

A. Because I had frequently seen her in his room before.

Q. You swear that was the reason of your curiosity; you had seen Mrs. Campbell there frequently be-
B fore?

A. Yes.

Q. What did you see?

A. I saw the Major laying along the foot of the bed, stark naked as he could be.
C   Q. Where was she?

A. She was sitting on the side of him with her hand upon his back.

Q. Was she drest or undrest?

A. She was drest.
D   Q. Had he no shirt on?

A. No shirt on at all.

Q. Was he stark naked?

A. Yes.

Q. Did you continue long there?
E   A. I continued there for some minutes, and as I stood there, Mrs. Campbell took her hands and drawed the curtain at the foot of the bed—I went down stairs.

Q. Did that prevent you seeing any thing else?
F   A. Yes.

Q. When the curtain was drawn and he was laying stark naked with his face to the bed, you went away?

A. Yes.
G   Q. Where do you live at present?

A. I live with Mr. Campbell's brother.

Q. Did you see any thing else at that time?

A. No, Sir, but I have heard say—

(99)

Cross-examined by Mr. Burrow.

Q. What time of the day was this?
A. As near as I can tell about 11 o'clock.
Mr. *Erskine.* This was at East Bourne?
A. At East Bourne.
Q. Do you know whether he had been bathing?
A. Yes, the Major had been bathing, but she had not.
Q. This was when he returned from the sea?
A. Yes, Sir.
Mr. *Burrow.* At eleven in the morning?
A. About eleven.
Q. What other servants were there in the house?
A. There was Flora and Maria.
Q. Had Mrs. Campbell been out that morning?
A. She had been out, I was not with her.
Q. What was the state of her health at East Bourne?
A. Often complaining of illness.
Q. Were Flora and the other woman the only women in the house?
A. Yes, Sir.
Q. Where are they?
A. I cannot tell.

Miss Macaulay *sworn.—Examined by Mr.* Erskine.

Q. Be so good as to tell us whether you are acquainted with Captain Campbell and his wife?
A. Yes, Sir, I am.
Q. Do you remember the time when Captain Campbell was preparing to go upon his voyage to India with his regiment?
A. I do.
Q. Do you know whether it was intended at that time Mrs. Campbell should accompany him?
N 2
A. I do

A A. I do not.

Q. How long was you acquainted with them ?

A. I knew her before she was married.

Q. Did you know her after she was married ?

A. Yes.

B Q. Did you know her soon after—was you in the habits of intimacy with her after she was married ?

A. Yes, Sir, she was some months with me.

Q. Did you see any thing improper in her behaviour during that time ?

C A. I never saw any thing improper in her behaviour.

Mr. *Erskine.* Q. Do you remember who she was left with ? In whose care was she left when the Captain went away ?

D A. She was at her mother's house in Brook-street, I think so.

Mr. *Erskine.* I rest it here for the plaintiff.

Cross-examination of Miss Macaulay.

E Q. Did you see much of Captain Campbell and his lady together ?

A. No, Sir.

Q. Very little, I fancy ?

A. Very little.

Q. So little as not to be able to form any idea of
F what terms they were living upon ?

A. I had not such frequent opportunities of seeing them.

Mr. *Erskine.* I have done, unless it should be necessary to give evidence in reply.

Mr. *Bearcroft*. May it pleafe your Lordſhip—— A
Gentlemen of the Jury, the evidence which has been
given on the part of the plaintiff intitles me to your
full and patient hearing. My title I put upon the
circumſtances that the cauſe as it now ſtands is of a
nature and of a complexion that muſt ſtrike every B
mind as undoubtedly a very aggravated caſe, and it
is of conſequence that every good mind will allow,
when ſuch a caſe is proved, that thoſe who are to decide upon it ſhould well weigh and conſider it, in order that that judgement, which they ultimately ſhall C
give, may be temperate and moderate, for unleſs it
be temperate and moderate, it cannot be juſt.

. Gentlemen, I ſhould not be entitled to a moment's
attention from you if I attempted to diſſemble reſpecting the weight which I feel upon my ſhoulders. D
The caſe which has been proved upon the part of the
plaintiff, has been ſtated, and muſt be ſtated, upon
this evidence, in two very ſtrong words, a caſe of
inceſt and adultery. I admit it, and I allow that ſuch
a caſe calls ſeriouſly upon the feelings of thoſe that E
hear it, and thoſe that are to determine upon it ; but
it is my duty to remark to you, and it will be the
principal remark with which I ſhall trouble you, to
diſtinguiſh the ſituation in which you are placed there ;
you are not put there, nor does my Lord ſit there, F
as I am ſure he will tell you, to puniſh the defendant
criminally for any crime or any offence : perhaps it
may be thought an opprobrium on the common law
of England, to ſay, it entertains no criminal juriſdiction for puniſhing ſuch offences either of adultery G
or inceſt ; but you all know very well there are different departments of different diſpoſitions as to the
power of puniſhing in different courts of different
deſcriptions, becauſe the common law has no ſuch
juriſdiction ; do not let it be thought by any one that
 3 ſuch

A such offences cannot be punished in England; for it is certain they may, and seriously too ; but that jurisdiction is an ecclesiastical jurisdiction, and not in common law courts.   I venture to remark, that not to defend simply the common law from imputation,

B that may arise in the mind at first view, to suppose it takes no notice of such conduct, but to remark that there is a place where the criminal part, and that only, is to be considered.

Gentlemen, my Lord will tell you the question in

C this cause, (for I am bound to tell you I do not mean to trouble you with witnesses in a cause of this kind) the only question will be, the damages you are to give—what is the satisfaction you are to make by your verdict for the plaintiff.

D   Gentlemen, when I am endeavouring to guard you against mixing and joining together the jurisdiction you have, not of the trial of a criminal offence with the jurisdiction you have, that of ascertaining civil damages which you are to give to the parties.   I de-

E sire to be understood as not to be contending for so absurd a doctrine as that you are to divest yourselves of all attention to that kind of case, and not to take it as matter of aggravation : but permit me to say it, and I do say it, because I think (and I do submit to

F the direction of the learned and noble Judge) that you are not, that you ought not, and that you have no power in the situation in which you stand, to give that which I know sometimes is called vindictive damages.   Vengeance and punishment of the crime

G belongs to another jurisdiction—you will take care in the verdict that you shall pronounce, that you will not by any means mix punishment which you have no right to take any notice of, upon the present occasion, with the question of damages you are to give to the parties.

Gentl

Gentlemen, it was faid in the outfet, it was under- **A**
ftood the counfel for the defendant would infift upon
the innocence of the defendant, and impute a good
deal of what you have heard to-day to the effects of
perjury.

Gentlemen, no power, no perfuafion, after the **B**
evidence given to-day, fhould prevail upon me to
ftand up as counfel for the party, to attempt to do
any thing of the kind. It never entered into the
mind of the defendant to give any fuch inftructions;
it would have been groffly abfurd to have done fo :— **C**
it would have been an additional load, I confefs, at
prefent I feel it is a heavy one; but I fhould then be
put in this condition, in endeavouring to quit the defendant, I fhould charge the plaintiff with a foul and
a black confpiracy, without any foundation of truth, **D**
and with bringing fuch a charge againft the defendant
and fupporting it by a variety of fuborned and per-
jured witneffes. My client difclaims any fuch idea—
fo much, therefore, as fuch an item, and it is a large
one defalcates from the damage that might have been **E**
given; I claim upon the part of the defendant.

Gentlemen of the Jury, having faid this, and
marked the line which feparates trial and punifhment
in a criminal court from the queftion of civil damages,
I am under the neceffity of chiefly relying upon that, **F**
and fubmitting it to his Lordfhip.

With regard to the damages, I have but a few, a
very few obfervations to make and to fubmit to your
cool judgement and obfervation.—The plaintiff quitted his wife, went to the Eaft Indies, and left her **G**
here. It has been attempted to bring a witnefs to
prove he intended to carry her with him—as far,
therefore, as that is an ingredient I call upon you
for a piece of juftice, to obferve that is not proved.

I prefs my obfervation further, I fay I have a right **H**
to afk of you, and in fuch a caufe you will not refufe

A it; I have a right to afk of you to conclude, that the clear fact is, that Mr. Campbell, the plaintiff, did not mean to take his wife with him, but to leave her here, for if he had any defire to take her with him, nothing upon earth was fo eafy to have done.

B   With regard to the manner in which the parties lived together, I cannot help obferving to you, there is not that full and fatisfactory proof that might be expected in a cafe of this fort. Perfons who might have been called, who were related and near relations

C to the plaintiff, the fervants and others are omitted to be called, which feems to leave that liable to fome degree of fufpicion; however you will not underftand me to be preffing it more than is neceffary. I admit there is fome evidence of their living together,

D and, perhaps, my Lord will tell you, when fome evidence is given of that, and it is not contradicted, it muft be taken; fuch was the fituation of the plaintiff and his wife, and in juftice you muft fo take it.

With regard to the damages, which is the only
E queftion before you, there is another circumftance which juries, during my experience in the profeffion, have been always taught to look to, becaufe it is effential they fhould, I mean the fituation and ability of the party in point of fortune. My learned friend,

F who never forgets, even in the outfet of the caufe, to ftate his client's cafe with all the advantages that belong to it, though fometimes he referves the ftrongeft powers for a reply, told you that the defendant in this cafe was a perfon who had refided many years in

G India, and was returned to Europe with a great fortune, a defcription as would defcribe Lord Clive, Mr. Barwell, or Mr. Sykes, and many of thofe perfons we are in the habit of calling Nabobs. Alas! that defcription very little fuits my client, which you can

H hardly doubt, becaufe there is not a tittle of evidence given, nor a queftion afked about his circumftances;
and

and my learned friend has finished his cafe. Now **A** as to that he is a Major, he has returned here moft undoubtedly originally with a few thoufands in his pocket, of a great part he prefently got rid here : he is about, and was about, to return to refume his fituation in the army in the Eaft Indies. **B**

It is in evidence before you he has three children, innocent perfons—they can be guilty of nothing—that is a circumftance in affeffing damages againft the father, which fathers, as fome of you are, I truft can never be prevailed upon totally to forget. **C**

Gentlemen, with thefe obfervations, therefore, I muft furrender the cafe, again I fay, to your temperate and moderate breaft—I fhall call no witneffes, for the reafons I have ftated—you are in poffeffion of the cafe—you will recollect, as I have faid, you are **D** not trying this man for crimes and offences, but to afcertain the damages that fuch a perfon as this fhall pay the plaintiff, under all the circumftances that belong to the cafe.

Gentlemen, the doctrine I take the liberty of pref- **E** fing upon you at this moment, is the doctrine of good fenfe and natural juftice.—It is the doctrine I take the liberty of faying, with fubmiffion to my Lord, the peculiar doctrine of the law of England. We know perfectly well that it is ftated by great authority, and **F** we read it in all the books—that an attention fhall be paid in the queftion of damages, nay even of criminal damages and fines, to the ability of the party to pay it—as to that in this cafe you are left to guefs at it—nothing is proved upon the part of the plain- **G** tiff, but that this gentleman has refided fome time here fince his return to Europe—though many return from India with great fortunes, many more return without them.

This is the cafe I have a right to make ; having **H** been diligent and careful not to ftate any thing improper, I hope and truft I have fucceeded, becaufe

O   moft

A moſt undoubtedly I ſhould be ſhocked, if in a cauſe of this ſort I was, in defending a man upon the article of damages, to do any thing to add to them. I appeal again to your moderate temper and juſtice.

B   *Lord Chief Juſtice.*—Lord Kenyon.

Gentlemen of the Jury, you muſt remember it is between four and five years ſince it has been a painful part of my duty too often to aſſiſt juries, as far as C I was capable of giving them any aſſiſtance, and to aſſiſt parties, that juſtice might be done. I was in great hopes the morals of the people would have totally extinguiſhed theſe kind of tranſactions; if it had it would have given great comfort indeed to me, D for I proteſt I never had ſerious cauſes of this kind come before me, without my feeling extremely for the diſtreſs of the party that applied to the laws of the country to obtain ſatisfaction for the injury received.

The prudent, diſcreet, and manly way in which E the learned gentleman who is juſt ſet down left the cauſe of his client, delivers me from the painful taſk of dragging through all that horrible ſtory the witneſſes have been examined to. It is admitted the caſe is proved and the plaintiff entitled to your verF dict—and the ſole conſideration is the quantum of damages he has received; and you have been put in mind, and very properly ſo, that this civil action is not a proceeding to puniſh the party as having been guilty and coming within any part of the criminal G law of this country—but when you are called upon merely to apportion damages to the injury he has received, I hardly know how I can tell you to meaſure that ſatisfaction in pounds, ſhillings, and pence. There are certain caſes in which ſome other mode of H proceeding is to be adopted by juries, which their good ſenſe will lead them to better than any directions I can preſume to give them, in actions brought
for-

forwards against persons of unfullied honour and A
character—it may be said in that case no damages
could be given, because such character is unaffaible
by the tongue of calumny. Gentlemen, the person
who takes my purse, is said by a very able writer to
take from me that which has been slave to thou- B
fands; but he that filches from me my good name,
robs me of that which not enriches him, but makes
me poor indeed. Whether this kind of injury may
not be referred to something of that kind is for you
to judge.—I will barely call to your attention the C
main outlines of this cause. The fituation of the
parties—what the plaintiff enjoyed, and that which
the plaintiff has loft by means of the defendant.
You were told in the outfet, this was a match in confequence of moft ardent affection; that it was a love D
match as far as fituation was difclofed, as far as we
reached they lived in the greateft harmony and comfort till he went to India, and it was then done away
in the manner you have heard; but it was hinted
fomething wrong happened in leaving his lady be- E
hind him on his going to India. What, then, Gentlemen, has every young officer that is called from
his family the means of doing it? Will the funds he
is in poffeffion of enable him to carry with him all
the comforts he has left behind him? And if he is F
torn away with a bleeding heart from thofe comforts,
is he to lofe them for ever? Are there no hopes of his
being received in the arms of his wife he affectionately loves when he comes back? Where could he
leave her in better when he went abroad, but in G
the houfe of her own mother? What! had he not a
right to expect from the neareft and deareft call of
nature, that an uncle, who was the brother of her own
mother, fhould affift her that wanted the immediate
protection of her hufband? But has fhe received that H
protection? I have a right to appeal to the evidence
given—is there not evidence of the confeffion of this

man,

A man, who told her she was a whore, a damn'd whore, and the worst of whores; she tells him that if she was a whore, she became a whore through his means, that she was his whore only; that he ought to have been her father and protector, but he has been the
B worst of enemies to her, and been the ruin of her family, and herself; alas, my poor husband!—Did she fall into the arms of this incestuous man? We find all possible means taken to corrupt her mind: books and prints to enflame the passions, too bad to
C be exhibited to any body, are exhibited by the uncle at a more advanced time of life to his own niece, the wife of another man.

Gentlemen, it is very true, in assessing damages of this kind, one would wish that they should be ap-
D portioned in some measure to the circumstances of the party who is to pay them. What his situation is I do not know; I do not know the situation of either of the parties, but poverty is no answer to a call of this kind, made by a man injured to the extent this
E man has been; I can point out no rule to you; there is no rule but that which has been suggested; you are certainly to consider it with temper and moderation: but at what sum, temper and moderation in a case of this sought ought to stop, is not for me to
F judge, but for you. I do not know how to adjust it. It stands distinct to the disadvantage of this defendant from all the causes I ever heard before—this seems to have been a plan to ruin the lady by the person who was this incestuous paramour.—It is for
G you to consider of your verdict.

[*The Jury retired some time, and brought in their Verdict for the Plaintiff—Damages £.3000.*]

Extract

Extract from the BON TON MAGAZINE *for* *February* 1793.

Subſtance of the ſingular Trial of Major Hook for crim. con. &c. before Lord KENYON, in the King's Bench, Tueſday, Feb. 26, 1793.

See the Plate entitled " The Marrow-bone Uncle, &c."—And for a tête-à-tête of the parties, turn to the firſt article in this number, which was printed off before the event of this trial was known.

LOVE AND INCEST;

OR THE

AMOROUS UNCLE AND THE WANTON TRAVELLER.

THERE is nothing, perhaps, in which the boaſted ſuperiority of man over the female part of the creation is marked with a blacker dye, than the impunity it affords him in the commiſſion of crimes which ſtain the character of a woman with everlaſting infamy; one falſe ſtep, one deviation from the path of virtue, ruins her for ever; while, on the contrary, her ſeducer is conſidered as having done nothing which deſerves the cenſure of ſociety.

The paſſions of the female ſex are known to be altogether as ſtrong, if not ſtronger, than thoſe of men; but for the credit of feminine modeſty, it muſt be owned that even while the fire of natural deſires rages in every part, it ſeldom happens that women can ſo far out-ſtrip the modeſty of nature as to
make

make the firft advances.—Men, who know as well their wifhes as their fears, are nine times in ten the firft aggreffors, they infinuate frefh poifon into the blood already inflamed, and they fmother the fentiment, as well as the apprehenfion which otherwife would preferve virtue.

This is a fact too notorious to be dwelt upon or denied, and, notwithftanding what may fometimes be faid in ridicule or in praife of the afcendancy, it certainly will not admit of philofophical juftification.

But, however we may now and then fpeak either lightly or warmly upon the of fubject feduction, in the regular and natural indulgence of irregular, though natural defires; however we may delineate the advances of love ; however tenderly we may tint the foft approaches to enjoyment ; and however highly we may colour the ecftacies of mutual indulgence, when no unnatural bar is caft between the intoxicated voluptuaries ; we muft at all times condemn that hateful concupifcence which gratifies its loofe paffions at the expence of nature.

The hero of our prefent tale, and a melancholy tale it is, had been many years a Major in the fervice of the Eaft India Company, and as a foldier and private gentleman always conducted himfelf with becoming propriety—He is faid to have faved an immenfe fortune in India, and was known to have returned home with a view of fpending the evening of his life in tranquillity : the heroine is his own niece, and in point of years might be his grand-child. In addition to the repulfive qualities of age, nature has been to the former unkind and niggardly, his perfon is rather difgufting than pleafing—In addition to the fafcinating powers of youth, to the latter, the goddefs has been profufe of her choiceft gifts; fhe is rather lovely than beautiful. The firft is, we are told, an old bachelor, the latter a matron, and united

to

to one of the moſt accompliſhed and conciliating men in Europe—He is a Captain in the Britiſh ſervice, and highly eſteemed, not only on account of his profeſſional, but his private excellence.

The parties are all natives of Scotland, where it unfortunately happened that Captain C—p—ll, our heroine's huſband, had ſome buſineſs to tranſact, which could not be executed but by himſelf or his frail mate ; the duties of his profeſſion prevented him from undertaking ſo long a journey, and as the Major, who ſupported a parental intercourſe in the family, was an idle man, it was propoſed that he ſhould accompany his niece to Edinburgh : what ſuſpicion could poſſibly reach to ſuch nearneſs of blood ? what ideas of indelicacy even could ariſe from a journey between two perſons ſo allied by conſanguinity, ſo ſeparated by years and perſonal diſparity ?

The time of departure being fixed, every thing was prepared, and the day of departure being arrived, the Captain himſelf handed his weeping wife into the carriage, and not without ſome ſympathetic emotions wiſhed her and her parental guardian a pleaſing journey, and a ſafe return.

It is remarked by writers of great reputation, and indeed it is a univerſal and natural obſervation, that if old women be not objects of deſire in the eyes of young men, old men cannot by the ſame parity of reaſon, be objects of deſire in the eyes of young women. How, therefore, to account for the gallantries which almoſt immediately took place between our amorous travellers is more than we can poſſibly glance at ; but the moſt probable ſuggeſtion is, that the firſt advances took place when they were both locked in the arms of ſleep, and that the " *fancy's midwife*" had painted things as they really were not— that the antiquated hero forgot that he was an uncle, and that the longing heroine conceived her hoary

I   com-

companion to be a Hercules. In which character it is not at all improbable but her warm imagination might have formed something like a club; at which, under the delusions of vision, she might have made an involuntary grasp.—Some such accident must have expedited the business, for certain it is, that even before they left the postchaise, the club was reduced to a distaff.

So very much delighted were these amorous relatives with the issue of the chaise adventure, that they repeated it at night in another situation. In fact, they never slept asunder during the whole journey, and so little caution did they adopt in the progress of their indulgence, that every chambermaid on the road saw them in situations of the most tender and critical description.

The Mutton Bone incident, as described in the plate, took place after the adventure in the coach, and fully accounts for the archness with which she receives her portion of the *marrow*.

Upon their arrival at Edinburgh, the lovers were not at all less cautious; and so public was the connection, that the Captain was soon acquainted with it; affecting, however, to be totally ignorant, he laid his plan so well, that he *stole a march*, and, like an old soldier, surprized the enemy literally *in the trench!*

Upon being thus surprized, 5000l. was immediately offered as a ransom, but the Captain thinking the Court of King's Bench, with Lord Kenyon, *and a Jury of twelve uncles, husbands, and friends, will deem that sum very inadequate, has already commenced his action, and the issue will be produced in the course of next term.*

ERRATA in the DEFENCE.

Page viii. line 13, for *misguided* read *misjudged*.

xl.   7, for *disagreeable* read *disgraceful*.

xli.   24, for *original witness* read *person not called*.

lv.   2, for *the conduct* read *to the conduct*.

lix.   6, for *tête-à-tête was* read *tête-à-tête which was*.

lxii.   17, for Capt. Campbell's letters see Appendix, p. 3.
C. D. p. 4. C. and p. 5. C.

lxv.   24, for *but found* read *but I found*.

www.ingramcontent.com/pod-product-compliance
Lightning Source LLC
Chambersburg PA
CBHW020538270326
41927CB00006B/638